High Percentage BASERUNNING

Harold S. Southworth

Leisure Press
Champaign, Illinois

Library of Congress Cataloging-in-Publication Data

Southworth, Harold S., 1925-
  High percentage baserunning / Harold S. Southworth.
    p. cm.
  Bibliography: p.
  Includes index.
  ISBN 0-88011-292-1
  1. Base running (Baseball).   2. Baseball—Coaching.   I. Title.
GV868.S68 1989
796.357'27—dc19   88-3668
                                                       CIP

ISBN: 0-88011-292-1

Developmental Editor: Sue Ingels Mauck; **Assistant Editors:** Robert King, Chris Drews; **Production Director:** Ernie Noa; **Typesetter:** Sandra Meier; **Text Design:** Keith Blomberg; **Cover Design:** Jack Davis; **Cover Photo:** Stephen Dunn/Focus West; **Illustrations By:** John Evanko and Mike McPhillips; **Printed By:** Versa Press

Printed in the United States of America   10 9 8 7 6 5 4

Leisure Press
A Division of Human Kinetics
Web site: http://www.humankinetics.com/

United States: Human Kinetics, P.O. Box 5076, Champaign, IL 61825-5076
1-800-747-4457
e-mail: humank@hkusa.com

Canada: Human Kinetics, Box 24040, Windsor, ON N8Y 4Y9
1-800-465-7301 (in Canada only)
e-mail: humank@hkcanada.com

Europe: Human Kinetics, P.O. Box IW14, Leeds LS16 6TR, United Kingdom
(44) 1132 781708
e-mail: humank@hkeurope.com

Australia: Human Kinetics, 57A Price Avenue, Lower Mitcham, South Australia 5062
(08) 277 1555
e-mail: humank@hkaustralia.com

New Zealand: Human Kinetics, P.O. Box 105-231, Auckland 1
(09) 523 3462
e-mail: humank@hknewz.com

To William and Hazel Southworth, my wife, Thelma,
and my children, Mike, John, and Kathy.

Contents

Foreword   vii

Preface   ix

Acknowledgments   xii

Chapter 1
The Components of Base Stealing   1

    Development of Rules and Base Stealing   1
    The Four Dimensions of Offense   2
    Positive and Negative Statistics in Baseball   3
    Statistics and Baserunning   3
    Misconceptions About the Running Game   4
    Consequences of Running Plays   6
    Factors That Influence Running Plays   6
    Baserunning Equipment   7

Chapter 2
Twenty-Eight Baserunning Plays   9

    Three Types of Running Plays   9
    How the Running Plays Were Evaluated   9
    Explanation of the Times of Runners and Throwers   13
    The 28 Plays   15

Chapter 3
The Official Rules of Running   73

    Section 7.0: The Runner   73
    Section 8.05: The Pitcher's Balk   85
    Section 10.08: When Is a Base Stolen?   86
    The Infield Fly Rule   86
    The First- and Third-Base Coach   87
    The Appeal Plays   87

Chapter 4
A Grand Tour of the Bases   89

    Tour 1: Running From Home Plate to First Base   89
    Tour 2: Running From First Base to Second Base   93
    Tour 3: Running From Second to Third Base   95
    Tour 4: Running From Third Base to Home Plate   96
    More Baserunning Tips   98
    The Catcher's Role   100
    Master Those Slides   100
    Six Methods of Getting the First Run of a Game   101

Chapter 5
Stealing Mechanics   105

    The Pitcher's Characteristics   105
    The Catcher's Characteristics   106

Game Situation: Count, Number of Outs, and Score 106
Which Base You Are Attempting to Steal 106
Making the Turn at First Base 107
The Elements of Stealing Second Base 108
The Elements of Stealing Third Base 111
How to Execute the Fake Steal Off First, Second, or Third
  Base 113
The Elements of Stealing Home 113

Chapter 6
The Hit Ball: What Runners Should Do   **117**

Use of the 36 Hit-Ball Charts 117
Running on Hit Ground Balls 117
Running on Fly Balls 118

Chapter 7
Baserunning Signs   **155**

The Total Number of Signs Required 155
Methods of Relaying Signs 155
The Take Sign 156
The Wipeoff Sign 156
When a Sign Is Misunderstood or Missed 157

Appendix: Play Selector   163
Glossary   169
Bibliography   173
References   175
Index   177

Foreword

Any baseball coach who believes in making things happen rather than waiting for them to happen should read this book. And even if you are a coach who believes in waiting for the big inning, I guarantee that after reading this book you will consider changing your style.

Stu Southworth has put together a scientific manual that takes away the guesswork and gives coaches exact percentages for their chances of success. He gives you the reasons for being confident in your offensive strategies—and as any baseball coach will tell you, confidence is the essential ingredient for teaching aggressive and intelligent baserunning.

This book is unique because it plots to the hundredth of a second—the exact time it takes the offense to execute a play and the defense to counteract it. Let me give you an example: To steal or not to steal? is the question every coach ponders as soon as a runner is aboard base. This book lists the time it takes for the pitcher to deliver the pitch and for the catcher to throw the ball, so that you can mathematically calculate your percentage of success. The only other information you need is the speed of your runner. After reading this book you will know that most offensive running plays are a question not of hoping the defense makes a mistake, but of simple mathematics. And Stu gives coaches 28 baserunning plays—all of them worthwhile.

The chapter on running rules (chapter 3) is a great idea; by combining that information with the chapter on the 36 types of hit balls (chapter 6) coaches and players can benefit greatly. Southworth's charts and diagrams make it easier for coaches and runners to make decisions during the game, saving valuable practice time and eliminating the trial and error that can be painful or damaging to your team. The Play Selector that Stu describes in the book's appendix is an excellent device for the young or inexperienced coach.

The charts and diagrams that Stu has included are also valuable teaching aids for conducting practices.

One or two charts can be posted daily in the dugout or clubhouse before practice and reviewed by the coach; then the team can take the field to practice the situations, both defensively and offensively, knowing in advance what to work on. Any team who did such practice for the course of a season would certainly be well schooled.

Jerry Kindall's analysis of running is a bonus for the reader. Both Stu and Jerry dispute the old myth that you cannot do anything to improve speed, emphasizing instead that running speed can indeed be improved with proper training and good techniques.

Throughout the book, small but important details are not overlooked. For example, Southworth explains that the batter/runner should, after striding past first base, "glance quickly over his right shoulder to see if the throw has gotten past the first baseman." This is a crucial instruction, one often neglected by coaches. How many times have you seen a runner get thrown out at second base or not even attempt to advance further because he discovers too late that the ball was overthrown?

Another example of Southworth's penchant for detail is his helpful tip that runners should slide into first base only when avoiding the tag. It is always quicker and safer to run through the bag, yet coaches often fail to mention this to their players.

Stu Southworth knows baseball and, in particular, baserunning. And I can testify that he practices what he preaches. When I was a high school player he coached in our league. His teams were always confident, aggressive, and well coached. I know that anyone who reads his book will be equipped to become a better coach and, in turn, to produce better teams.

Gary Adams
Head Baseball Coach
UCLA Bruins

Preface

Batting, or hitting, is rightly called baseball's first dimension of offense. Nearly every batter who steps up to the plate keeps one thought foremost in mind—to get a hit. And certainly there will never be a more important element of offense in the game of baseball. Yet this eagerness, this single focus, often leads to the assumption that the only way a team can win a game is to get base hits.

As I intend to show in every chapter of this manual, this assumption is incorrect. It has been disproven over and over by coaches and players who understand the runner's game—baseball's fourth dimension of offense.

In 1937 my father took me to see my first professional game—the San Diego Padres against the San Francisco Seals. He pointed out by name the great hitters, pitchers, infielders, and outfielders. Impressed by the reputation and prowess of those strong players, I remember even more vividly, however, my initial attraction to the runner's game—my fascination with the stolen base.

Later, as I gained experience playing baseball, I soon discovered I was not gifted with great speed—and so the running game took on a more personal significance. After more than 30 years as a coach, this focus has grown from a fascination to a systematic overview, a philosophy defended by records and statistics. My goal in writing this book is to show the importance of the runner's game as equal, or very nearly equal, to the other three dimensions of offense in the game of baseball.

Team-oriented baserunning, or stealing, has often been an overlooked, sometimes scorned, approach to advancing runners. But this fourth dimension of offense—the missing dimension, as I often call it—can win games when other strategies fail. Practiced systematically and comprehensively, it can be a consistently effective part of any team's offense. It can also add greatly to the challenge and excitement of the game.

Nearly every game presents countless opportunities to steal bases, score runs, and reduce the worst negative statistic in baseball: LOB—left on base. It is the purpose of this manual to help coaches and players become more keenly aware of these opportunities and to take full advantage of them.

Like everything else, the game of baseball has a history. In 1845, stealing played little if any role in the original sport Alexander Cartwright derived from the British game of rounders. But by 1890, the National League had developed and established the rules and regulations we use today. The result of much experimentation, these rules reflect the attainment of a nearly perfect balance between offense and defense. As defense improved over the initial three or four decades of the game, baserunning became more and more important.

As the sport evolved and rules tightened, coaches and players developed several plays to advance runners without the help of the batter's skill or luck in hitting the ball. My investigation shows that, to date, 28 plays have been devised. After almost 12 decades of professional ball, strong coaches at every level of the game understand the importance of baserunning and the need to incorporate as many of the plays as possible as part of regular training. On the other hand, several reasons are sometimes given for the neglect of fourth-dimension offense. From my point of view, all these reasons are misconceptions about the runner's game.

My approach to the essence and to the many facets of the runner's game is from three directions: historical, theoretical, and practical. In addition to the plays themselves, coaches, players, and fans need to know a little baseball history to fully appreciate the importance of fourth-dimension offense. This in-depth presentation is designed to provide a sound grasp of the various strategies for successful execution of all the plays and, I hope, provide some entertainment and enjoyment as well.

Chapter 1 presents an historical overview of the sport from its modest beginnings in mid-19th century America to the period following the Civil War. In just over two decades, the new game rose from obscurity to tremendous popularity. Soon afterward, it became a business, with professional managers and professional players.

As the game became more competitive and intense, baserunning became an important skill—and then a science. But coaches and managers soon split into several camps. Although some showed outright contempt for the stolen base, others coached a wide-open game, developing their own running styles and philosophies. Many others fell somewhere between the extremes. Chapter 1 traces the overall changes in the philosophy of fourth-dimension offense from 1860 to the present.

The first chapter also presents some revealing statistics on the game in general and on the running game in particular. Eight common myths about baserunning are described and debunked. Chapter 1 concludes with a general list of consequences of running plays plus a short section on baserunning equipment.

Chapter 2 continues the historical survey and presents a full breakdown of all the individual and team-running plays attempted since 1860. Each play is described, analyzed, and timed to the one tenth of a second. Recorded times of the runner and of the ball are compared. Stealing and/or scoring opportunities are pointed out in various playing situations, including steals before and after the pitcher's delivery, the hit-and-run play, the fake-steal play, and all the bunting and fake-bunting plays. A final section on defensive maneuvers includes a discussion of the intentional walk and instructions to catchers.

Chapter 3 offers a theoretical approach to baserunning, citing every rule from Section 7.0, "Running," from *Official Baseball Rules*. Each rule is followed by a simplified interpretation accessible to players of all ages and levels. After each explanation, two aids for learning and remembering the rule are given. The "Helpful Tips" sections explain how to gain greatest advantage from each rule and how to avoid specific pitfalls.

The drills sections of chapter 3 will be of prime importance to coaches at all levels of the game. So far as I know, these drills are original to baseball training and practice. I employed two coaches to help develop drills that show the runner all the dos and don'ts for each running rule. Players make many mistakes in game after game for the simple reason that they do not know the rules. Such blunders can be virtually eliminated by practice drills. Chapter 3 also presents rules on the pitcher's balk and the infield fly, then concludes with directions for appeal plays.

Chapter 4 begins with a guided tour around the bases in order to illustrate every play that could occur at each base. Runners are informed of any circumstance, standard or unorthodox, they might encounter. Dos and don'ts at each point, the use

of base coaches, and official rules are emphasized. Six strategies for scoring the first run of a game—an important trick—are also explained.

Chapter 5 provides insight into the various types of steals and the skills required to steal any one of the bases. Pitchers' and catchers' traits are studied carefully. This chapter also shows proper running form and body mechanics, explaining how to take turns around bases, lead off, hold up, slide, and run on an overthrown ball. The runner learns that running one of the bases is not the same as running either of the other two—different rules and techniques apply to each of the three bases.

Chapter 6 looks at the 36 types of balls that can be hit by the batter. Each of these is titled, analyzed, and charted according to what the runner should do in the case of no outs, one out, or two outs.

Chapter 7 provides a discussion of baseball's most sacred and mysterious ritual: coaching signs—signals to the runner and/or the batter. Various theories of sign-giving are included, along with discussions by coaches ranging from those who give fewer than six signs to those who employ every running play in the game. Two methods of relaying signals are presented. I also reveal my own long-kept secrets of sign-giving. Signs for each of the 28 plays are titled, defined, and illustrated.

In the appendix you will find a valuable tool for putting these plays to use: the play selector. This device allows you to have at your fingertips an organized listing of the appropriate plays for almost every game situation.

High Percentage Baserunning represents my contribution to a sport that has given me 48 years of challenge and enjoyment. It is my hope that this work will stimulate greater interest in baserunning and add new challenge for players and new excitement for fans of the sport that will remain our national pastime, a game now popular in many parts of the world. That room for improvement still exists after 142 years of change and refinement keeps me as enthusiastic as ever about the great game of baseball.

In the past 10 years, the art of baserunning has enjoyed a comeback, an intensification at the pro game level. This manual is written for all coaches and players, but particularly those at the middle levels of the game—Pony League, high school, and college ball clubs. It will also be useful to Little

League coaches, but strict rules related to leading off bases will limit baserunning tactics at this level.

Critics have often said the game of baseball is too slow and not exciting enough. Millions of fans and thousands of players probably do not agree—yet often, except for the batter at the plate, a team does seem simply to wait, to play passively, relying entirely upon the batter to get things moving on the field. Team-orchestrated baserunning, practiced seriously and consistently, injects a new level of action and excitement into every inning where it is attempted aggressively—and against which it is strongly defended.

So let's get moving—and start giving our players and our fans a real run for their money.

Acknowledgments

I would like to gratefully acknowledge the assistance of Gary Adams, Claude Anderson, Claude Monger, and Gordon Sloan for their contributions; Ella Penny, Mr. Sauer, Bob Webster, and Gordon Burgett for their encouragement; Jim McGarry for editing of the first draft; Jerry Kindall and the office of the Commissioner of Baseball for permission to quote from their publications; Freddie and Jim Spellacy for providing the office space in which to write this book; and Michelle Southworth, Pam Crosson, and Cecille Watkins for typing the manuscript.

I also want to thank the following coaches for returning questionnaires and providing me with their expertise and experience in baserunning: Jim O'Brien, Charles Griggs, Jess Angel, Ron Willis, Wayne Smith, Bill Havard, Tommy Thompson, Larry Longworth, Owen Wright, Lester Simpson, Gary Weiberg, and Joel Escobar.

1

The Components of Base Stealing

History implies an account of chronological events, but it literally means "an investigation for the purpose of understanding events or subjects." To fully understand the powerful role base stealing can play in the game of baseball, we need to investigate the development of fourth-dimension offense. In other words, we need to look briefly into the long history of the sport.

Development of Rules and Base Stealing

Abner Doubleday of Cooperstown, New York, is traditionally credited with inventing the game of baseball in 1839. But more reliable records suggest the credit should go to Alexander Cartwright, who derived the original sport from the British game of rounders that same year. In rounders, four stones or posts placed from 12 to 20 yards apart marked the corners of a square or diamond. Until about 1845 the game was played by many teams, with rules that varied from team to team and from region to region.

In 1845 Cartwright developed a set of standard rules, including a 90-foot distance between the bases. The ball was pitched underhand 45 feet from

home plate so that it could and would be hit. The game ended only when one team scored 21 runs, or aces. In this early version of the sport, base stealing was unimportant. But in 1858, with the formation of the National Association of Baseball Players, a period of experimentation with the rules began in an attempt to achieve a better balance between offense and defense.

From 1861 to 1865, Abner Doubleday distinguished himself as a major general in the Civil War. When he returned to civilian life, he must have been astonished to find his pastime grown so popular. In 1869 the Cincinnati Red Stockings became the first professional team—from that moment, the race was on.

Trial-and-error attempts to balance offense and defense intensified. After many experiments with different base distances, it became clear that the 90-foot standard established by Cartwright more than two decades earlier produced a very close play at any base the runner attempted to steal. It is remarkable that this distance seems to pit the fastest runner against the best throw a good catcher can make.

By 1890, the National League had developed a four-ball count for walks, a three-strike count for outs, a nine-inning game duration, and other rule changes that made baseball at the end of the 19th century almost identical to the game today. Of course, all these rule changes occurred because of increased competitiveness, improvements in defensive play, and the desire for more action.

As the rules changed, base stealing became a more important element in the game. Because the ball was no longer pitched to be hit, but to strike out the batter, the runners could not rely wholly on the batter to advance them. The new rules created a fairly even balance between the offensive challenge of the base runner and the defensive abilities of the pitcher, catcher, infielders, and outfielders.

The exact historical development of fourth-dimension offense has been lost, but as the game progressed, more and more plays were devised. No records were kept regarding the sequence of this evolution. My investigation shows that 28 primary plays have been invented to date.

The Four Dimensions of Offense

Offensive strategy in baseball can be divided easily into four categories or dimensions: (a) hitting, or batting; (b) receiving a walk to first base; (c) individual baserunning (stealing without help from the batter or another runner); and (d) team baserunning, a cooperative tactic involving two runners or the batter and one or more runners. This last or fourth dimension can be thought of as the formation of a team within a team.

The first, most obvious dimension of offensive strategy requires the batter to hit the ball to get on base. If, however, the pitcher throws more than three inaccurate balls, and the batter takes these pitches, or if the pitch hits the batter, then the batter enters the second dimension and walks to first base. If the batter bunts to get on first, then he adopts third-dimension tactics. Similarly, a runner acting individually to advance himself moves in the third dimension.

But it is in the dimension of team running, the fourth dimension of offense, that the most remarkable and innovative discoveries have been made on the diamond. The complexity of both orthodox and unorthodox plays presents a greater challenge to practice and learn baserunning as offense and, of course, as tactics to oppose in defense.

It is in this fourth dimension of offense, however, that ball clubs are sometimes inadequately prepared—and many coaches will freely admit it. Ardent fans know it, too. Yet, extra knowledge and skill in this area can give the offensive team just the polish and edge it often needs to win. Players working together on the bases as a team, or the batter and one or more runners coordinating their efforts—this is what I mean by the missing dimension in baseball today.

In the first few decades of the game, team running played a nominal role. But as the finer points of baseball evolved after 1869, various pro clubs tried different batter-runner combinations in an attempt to steal their way around the diamond. A good example is the standard hit-and-run play. In these early decades of the modern game, coaches recognized, to a greater or lesser degree, that the defense could not always react to the element of surprise.

Skillful base stealers create many advantages for their teams. A good base runner distracts the defensive players, especially the pitcher, who can lose his intensity and concentration on the batter. A good runner makes the defensive men play out of position, a shade over from their normal slots, creating holes through which the hit ball can be driven safely. An aggressive base stealer can cause the pitcher to commit a balk. He can break up double plays at the bases by beating the throw on a force-out or by upending the player attempting a throw to the next base.

His running skills can disorient the other team, causing the defense to guard constantly against the hit-and-run tactic or any number of other steal or delayed-steal plays. His speed, daring, and most of all his precise timing keep the entire infield guessing as to which play will be attempted next. And if he is not alone, but paired with the batter and/or another runner, a cunning base stealer will drastically change the defensive team's thinking and playing tactics.

Yet, historically, some managers have been reluctant to experiment beyond a handful of standard team-running plays.

With the slow development of fourth-dimension tactics, several myths about the runner's game also evolved, preventing adoption of the full repertoire by many clubs. These misconceptions divided the early world of baseball into two camps—the purists and the experimenters.

Before we examine and expose these myths in detail, however, I would like to present some essential and, I believe, eye-opening statistics on the overall game and the running game in particular.

Positive and Negative Statistics in Baseball

Examine any baseball scorebook and you will see that the game is one of many statistics. Probably in no other sport have as many statistics been kept as carefully. The kinds of information recorded can be divided conveniently into two categories: positive and negative statistics (Table 1.1).

Table 1.1 Positive and Negative Statistics in Baseball

Positive		Negative	
W	= Win	L	= Loss
R	= Runs	E	= Errors
H	= Hits	LOB	= Left on base
AB	= At bat	K	= Strikeouts
RBI	= Runs batted in	PB	= Passed ball
1B	= Single	WP	= Wild pitch
2B	= Double	BK	= Balk
3B	= Triple		
HR	= Home run		
BB	= Bases on balls (walks)		
HP	= Hit by pitcher		
SAC	= Sacrifice		
PO	= Putouts		
A	= Assists		
SB	= Stolen bases		
IW	= Intentional walk		

Of the negative statistics, certainly the most devastating to any team are these three: (a) errors, (b) strikeouts, and (c) left on base. Costly errors allow the opposition to score runs and can prolong an inning that should have ended. When the batter strikes out, another out is lost or another inning ended—but much worse, in my opinion, runners already on base will never be advanced to home.

It is one thing to get a man on base, but entirely another to move him along three more times to score a run. As he nears home plate, advancing him becomes progressively more difficult. Too many coaches rely too heavily on their hitters to move men already on base. From my viewpoint, LOB overshadows all other negative statistics by far. These men, if they had advanced, might have turned a loss into a victory.

Statistics and Baserunning

The average batter in baseball, including high school, college, and professional players, hits around .260. Given these odds, the coach places a one-out-of-four bet that the batter will advance his runners one or two bases. These odds are not too bad, one might argue.

Results from my investigation of the running game, however, produced statistics that make these odds look poor. When I began my coaching career in 1947-48, I decided to keep baserunning records for my high school and American Legion teams. For 37 years I compiled statistics on the success and failure rates of all running plays attempted in more than 630 games. Then in 1981 I set up an experiment to compare to the one tenth of a second the times required for all possible running maneuvers against the times of all possible defensive throws. To my complete surprise I found that in 80 percent of the plays, if executed correctly, the runner will beat the throw to the base—even if the defense does not make even one of 16 possible errors.

From the college level down to Little League, if the defense makes even one of these errors, the runner always advances to the next base. Overall, I found the percentage of success in most of the plays to be 50 to 80 percent. If we look at offensive strategy as a gamble against odds, a coach has four betting options to advance men on base:

1. Let the batter hit away in an effort to move the runner along. The odds are three to one against him.
2. From the repertoire of 28 plays, signal the runner to attempt a trick play if the batter does not hit the pitched ball. The percentage of success here is between 50 and 85 percent. The batter may hit the ball, thus negating a running play already begun.
3. Using one of the 28 plays, bet on the defense committing one of 16 possible errors. If this bet is good, the runner advances every time.

For example, the batter gets the take sign and one runner advances.

4. Choosing one of the 28 running plays, signal the batter to take the pitch. Here we put no money on the batter, placing all on the runner or runners. Again, chances for success in most of the plays average 50 to 80 percent. These are multiple-runner plays in which runners work together as a "team within a team."

In the last three cases, the odds for success are at least 50 percent better than in the first-dimension bet. Greater use of these alternatives to hitting could really turn the game around for many teams. Yet for 30 years or more I have heard the same song after a game. It goes like this: "Our pitcher pitched a great game and our defense was good, but we had 16 men left on base—we lost 3-2."

But the lyrics to this sad song aren't complete. No explanation is offered for the fate of those 16 men who ended up LOB. The truth is the coach did not prepare enough baserunning strategy to move at least four or five of those runners along one base more. Not only would the losing team have added to its score, but each time a runner advanced, a possible force play by the defense would have been eliminated. That philosophy of offense that *waits* for things to happen instead of *making* them happen often loses.

Probabilities of Scoring by Base Hits

Allowing for defensive errors and bases on balls, with an average of .260, the average hitter will get on base only three out of every ten tries, at most. The batter's overall odds, then, are about .300. Once he reaches first, however, his odds for scoring decrease with the number of outs against his team: with no outs, 70 percent will score; with one out, 30 percent will score; with two outs, only 15 percent will score.

Probabilities of Getting a Home Run

Several years ago I recorded all the times at bat for 100 high school teams over three seasons, a total of 75,000 times at bat. The percentage of home runs averaged between one and two percent. During those same years I kept identical records for both the American and National Leagues. About one percent of the total times at bat resulted in home runs.

Probabilities of Scoring by Sacrifice Bunting

Chances for success by this method depend on which base the runner holds and the number of outs. Moving a runner to second base by sacrifice bunting usually means giving up an out. With one out, the runner's chances of scoring from second are between 40 and 50 percent. If he is advanced to third base with one out, the odds for scoring increase to an even 50 percent. But if either runner is advanced with two outs, the odds drop to 30 percent.

Hope springs eternal in the human breast, true, but the odds are 98 to 1 against the hope that a home run will clear the bases of all your runners. Instead of hoping, why not take advantage of fourth-dimension offense?

Misconceptions About the Running Game

As a fly fisherman who loves to work the high streams of the West, I recall many encounters with fellow anglers at the end of a long day of wading and casting. With empty creel, the weary fly fisherman sometimes meets a young lad carrying a string of big trout. Naturally, the gentleman inquires about the bait the boy used. The answer is always the same: "Worms, sir," or sometimes "grasshoppers" or "hellgrammites."

But the gentleman only rolls his eyes and, letting out a sigh of exasperation, gets in his car and drives back to the city. He would never trade his hand-tied Eastern patterns for a messy insect. He prefers to lose his quest for the trout rather than adopt a method that will succeed. He is a *purist*.

A similar division of thought has prevailed throughout the history of baseball. The purist would rather rely on the bat—and on the home run in particular—rather than employ "lowly" baserunning tactics. Turning his nose up at the bunt and the stolen base, he waits patiently, doggedly, for the crack of the bat, the thrill of the home run to electrify the crowd. The purist believes that batting is the only true way to play the game. But the wait is often long, and often the game is lost.

I am not much of a purist in either baseball or fishing. I appreciate well-tied flies and home runs, but I also enjoy winning. Maybe if a big hatch is on, or if you happen to be Casey Stengel with Yogi Berra and other big hitters on your team, purism will prevail against all odds. But under less than ideal conditions, it is usually inadequate. Isn't the main purpose of stream fishing to catch trout? Isn't the main idea in the game of baseball to score runs?

Jackie Robinson, a great hitter, was also a good infielder and a cunning base runner. His versatility and flexibility represent my ideal. Contemporary players like Vince Coleman and Willie McGee of the St. Louis Cardinals and Rickey Henderson of the New York Yankees are also good examples of runners who know how to disrupt a game by stealing their way to success. Shouldn't there be many more such examples—at every level of the game? The great UCLA basketball coach, John Wooden, put it emphatically: "Coaches have success, then they lean on those methods that got them there, and they get lazy and fail to be innovative. They quit growing."

Maybe this is one reason why negative myths about the runner's game have persisted so long. In the discussion to follow, I will list the main objections coaches voice against a wide-open running game. For each of these viewpoints, I will offer a rebuttal based on my coaching experience of 630 games. I would like to explode these myths and win some converts to a more active, more dynamic game of baseball.

Fallacy 1: *Only the bat should be used to score men who got on base by the use of the bat. The bunt or stolen base is too risky; outs must be guarded carefully. The gamble of stealing is too great.*

Rebuttal: Such conservatism fails to realize that for each base stolen, the defense loses a possible double play by forceout, and that all runners move into scoring position. Statistical odds for competent runners are in favor of baserunning. Nothing ventured—nothing gained.

Fallacy 2: *To teach 28 running plays will take too long and only confuse the average player. Most players are not intelligent enough to learn and remember all the plays.*

Rebuttal: Rare as it is to see a team able to execute all 28 plays, this does not mean the full number

cannot be taught. The player will not be confused if (a) he is of average intelligence, (b) the plays are taught slowly and often and the number is increased gradually, and (c) the coach believes in his methods and can show players how all plays can succeed in game situations. Motivation and incentive are big factors here.

Fallacy 3: *If baserunning is emphasized, players will minimize or neglect other parts of the game.*

Rebuttal: This will not be the case if the coach impresses upon his players the equal importance of all dimensions of offense. *With one practice per week devoted completely to baserunning*, and all other sessions concentrated on the other elements of the game, there will be no overemphasis in game situations.

Fallacy 4: *The best way to win is to keep it simple. Complexity creates conflict.*

Rebuttal: If we keep it simple, then we have a simple team. Situations in almost every game call for a diversity of offensive strategy—but the simple team will lack options. A team with 10 good running plays will have a distinct advantage over one with only 4 or 5.

Fallacy 5: *Only a bunch of speed demons could make all those plays really work.*

Rebuttal: Eleven decades of baseball have proven that smart base runners can beat fast but not-so-smart base runners. Speed, of course, is an important factor, but not as great as intelligence. How much to lead off a base, when to go, how far down the line to go on a hit ball, and when to take the extra base are as critical—or more so—as speed.

Fallacy 6: *"At Good Old State University we won the league title without any fancy running or bunting plays—who needs them?" Fancy baseball is not true baseball.*

Rebuttal: New coaches often feel they must adhere to methods used by their coaches, particularly if the old coach was successful. But hero worship can impede growth and, in new situations, lose games. For years, old diehard players and fans have berated the running game and all the trickier plays possible on the diamond, even calling it "little ball." This is purism at its most elevated form.

Former pro players are especially guilty of this highbrow attitude. In most cases, plays that might indeed fail if attempted in major league games will work well at lower levels.

Fallacy 7: Everyone will think we're crazy to try these weird plays.

Rebuttal: Young coaches sometimes fear to try anything outside mainstream, orthodox tactics such as the hit-and-run or sacrifice bunt plays. Probably they are afraid to risk calling an unfamiliar play in front of fans, players, and other coaches. But when fans witness the added excitement these plays can bring, they will respond enthusiastically.

Fallacy 8: Practice time spent on the 28 baserunning plays will not pay off.

Rebuttal: If emphasized as important, conducted in an organized manner, and made to be fun, practice time will more than pay for itself. *Just one practice session per week devoted to these plays will be adequate to greatly improve any team's running game.*

Before going to the field, however, a general discussion of running theory should be presented to players before they analyze and practice individual plays. They need to know, in general, what they must do and what can happen during any attempt to steal.

Consequences of Running Plays

Below is a list of runners' responsibilities and a catalogue of possible, and even probable blunders by the six infielders. It should be remembered that, initially, the runner is at a disadvantage, for he must react to the pitcher before delivery. After the pitch, however, the defense assumes the more difficult task, for it is vulnerable to no less than 16 possible errors and must be prepared to react to any one of these mistakes.

What a Runner Must Do During a Running Play

- Receive and understand the correct sign from the coach.
- Get correct lead off base.
- Play dumb and be an excellent actor.
- Break at exactly the correct time. Timing must be precise.
- Run as hard as he can.
- Slide low into the bag.
- Slide correctly, being careful not to overslide the bag.
- Remember whether to make slide to inside or to outside.
- In a rundown situation, force the defense to make many tosses and avoid being tagged as long as he can, until all runners advance a maximum distance.
- Be ready to advance in case of a misplay by defense.

What Might Happen to the Defense

- Pitcher may balk.
- Pitcher may hit the batter.
- Pitcher may wild pitch.
- Catcher may cause passed ball.
- Catcher may interfere with the batter.
- Catcher may drop the ball.
- Catcher may fumble the ball.
- Catcher may hesitate before his throw.
- Catcher may throw wildly to the base.
- Baseman may forget to cover.
- Baseman may make a poor tag.
- Baseman may miss the tag.
- Baseman may drop the ball.
- Baseman may hesitate before throwing to another base.
- Baseman may throw wildly to the next base.
- Baseman in a rundown play may lob the ball or bobble the ball and fail to tag the runner or to throw in time to get another runner.

Although skilled defensive players might be expected to make few mistakes, the surprise and pressure of a baserunning play can cause the defense to err even on simple skills. The probability of an error by the defense is often greater than the probability of the runner being tagged or thrown out.

Factors That Influence Running Plays

Each of these factors will be described briefly here. More detail will be provided in later chapters.

- *Condition of the playing field:* Wet fields, or weather conditions such as cold or wind, will slow a runner. Some playing surfaces may not be in good shape. Coaches and runners are wise to consider these negative factors.
- *Speed of the runners:* Speed is the one factor that a coach cannot coach against. Raw speed will steal bases on the best pitchers and catchers. Holding the runner on base by the pitcher is the best defense.
- *Pitcher's time for delivery:* This varies greatly with pitchers. Time needed to release the ball from the beginning of stretch or windup will affect a runner's chances on a play. Study each pitcher to determine this.
- *Lead-off distance:* Each runner should know his maximum lead-off distance. Usually, it is 14 feet maximum in high school ball. Faster runners can extend this distance, as can the great professional runners.
- *Catcher's throwing ability:* This is a very important factor, but it can be negated by a pitcher's slow delivery or a slower type of pitch to the batter. All runners must study the catcher's throwing arm, quick release time, and accuracy.
- *Outs, innings, runs, count on the batter, and the score:* These are critical factors. Unless the runner has been given the green light to run on his own, the coach or manager will determine the pitch to steal on. Generally, this is not the runner's responsibility.
- *Number of runners on the bases:* If another man is on the base ahead of him, of course the runner cannot steal the next base. Also, certain plays require that a runner or runners be on particular bases. When a runner is not the only man on base, he should review in his mind those plays he has practiced with that combination of runners and look for signs for those possible plays.

Baserunning Equipment

A base runner must have several important pieces of personal equipment. These include a good set of sliding pads, thick and long enough, a good pair of spiked baseball shoes, and a set of running gloves. Although today's baseball uniforms are more formfitting, sliding pads are still an essential item of safety equipment. A team that does a lot of running is going to do a great deal of sliding and make some body contact with defensive players. Any padding will help. One bad slide, one head-on collision on the base paths, one painful "strawberry" can put a ball player out of action for weeks.

Select thick sliding pads that fit correctly. They should tie down, not slip on or be held by elastic, except for the band at the bottom of the pad. The padding should cover the side of the leg up to the hipbone and above, protecting the muscle area and all points where bones protrude. The sliding pad should curve around the side of the leg and over part of the leg in front, and in back it should cover part of the buttocks. The pads should fit snugly but should not restrict running movement or speed. Choose the sliding pads carefully and keep them in good repair.

In selecting baseball shoes, a good runner wants the longest, sharpest spikes the rules will allow. It is essential that shoes tie and fit snugly, but not too tightly. In trying to dig in and get that fast first step, runners want maximum traction. Only shoes with long spikes will provide this.

The usual selection of hitting gloves is adequate for sliding and running. A runner wants his gloves to fit tightly and cover the whole hand. Most of these gloves close and tighten with Velcro pads. They can be purchased in all colors, to match uniforms. Choose fairly thick gloves, because their purpose is to prevent hand injuries from abrasive sliding and from being stepped on, spiked, or hit on the hand by a thrown ball. An injured hand could keep a player out of the lineup for a long time.

If you are now more interested in the running game than before, and if your bias against it—if you had one—has lessened a little, let's move on to the challenge and beauty of the plays themselves.

2

Twenty-Eight Baserunning Plays

Twenty-eight principal plays comprise the total of running plays devised since modern baseball began over a century ago. This chapter will categorize and present the major plays one by one so that anyone can study and understand them—or teach them.

Three Types of Running Plays

Type 1: Plays in this category are classified according to the positions of the base runners: (a) no one on, (b) man on first, (c) man on second, (d) man on third, (e) men on first and second, (f) men on second and third, (g) men on first and third, and (h) bases loaded.

Type 2: These plays are classified according to the time of execution: before, during, or after the pitcher's delivery.

Type 3: Plays in this group are classified by the kinds and combinations of offensive players involved: (a) the batter alone, (b) a single runner, (c) the batter working with one or two runners, and (d) two runners working together without the batter. Tables 2.1, 2.2, and 2.3 group all of baseball's running plays into the appropriate categories or types.

How the Running Plays Were Evaluated

When I began my coaching career in 1947-48, I decided to keep baserunning records both for my high school and my American Legion teams. Many of the findings presented in this chapter are derived from these 37 years of statistics covering more than 630 games.

At the beginning of my first high school season in Silver Lake, Washington, I drew up a chart entitled "Percentage of Success for Baserunning Plays." Opposite the title of the play in the far left column, four columns indicated the basic statistics for each play: *Tried, O.K., Fail,* and *Percentage of Success.* I completed a chart for each game of the season.

After each game I posted the chart as an incentive and encouragement to my players. And at the end of each season I calculated the percentage of success for each play over the course of the entire season. When I retired recently from coaching, I tallied all the plays for all the games I had coached and arrived at overall percentages of success based on the large, long-term sample.

Table 2.1 Baserunning Plays Broken Down by the Positions of Runners on Various Bases

Special situation	Name of play	Man on 1st	Man on 2nd	Man on 3rd	Men on 1st and 2nd	Men on 2nd and 3rd	Men on 1st and 3rd	Bases loaded	Nobody on base
Before pitcher delivers	Double steal			X (Batter walks)			X (any # of outs)		
While pitcher is delivering	Single steal	X	X	X		X	X (any # of outs)		
	Double steal				X				
	Triple steal							X	
After the pitcher has delivered (catcher has the ball)	Double steal (men on 1st and 3rd only)						X (any # of outs)		
	Delay steal		X	X	X	X		X	
None	Hit and run play	X	X		X		X		
None	Fake steal	X	X	X	X	X	X	X	
Batter has intention of bunting	Drag bunt (for base hit)	X	X	X	X	X	X		X
	Sacrifice bunt (move runner one base)	X	X		X		X		
	Sacrifice bunt (move runner two bases)	X							
	Safe-squeeze bunt			X		X	X		
	Suicide squeeze (score one run)			X		X	X	X	
	Suicide squeeze (score two runs)					X		X	
Fake bunts	Fake bunt and slash	X	X	X					
	Fake bunt	X	X						

In 1981, I decided to refine my statistical analysis by determining to the one tenth of a second the time required for the 24 possible throws made by defense against the 28 stealing maneuvers. Using a stopwatch again, I also recorded the time for the 17 different runs made by men executing the 28 plays. I then compared the times of the ball or throw with the times of the runner for each play. I was totally surprised to find that *in 80 percent of the plays, the runner will beat the throw to the base.*

Table 2.2 Baserunning Plays Broken Down by Timing Before, During, and After the Pitcher's Delivery

Name of play	Before pitcher delivers	During pitcher's delivery	After pitcher delivers (catcher has the ball)
Double steal (men on 1st and 3rd)	X		
Double steal (men on 1st and 3rd—2 outs)	X		
Double steal (man on 3rd, batter walks)	X		
Single steal (man on 1st)		X	
Double steal (men on 1st and 2nd)		X	
Triple steal (bases loaded)		X	
Single steal (man on 3rd or 2nd)		X	
Double steal (men on 1st and 3rd)		X	
Double steal (men on 1st and 3rd—2 outs)		X	
Double steal (men on 1st and 3rd)			X
Double steal (men on 1st and 3rd—2 outs)			X
Delay steal (man on 2nd)			X
Delay steal (men on 1st and 2nd)			X
Delay steal (men on 2nd and 3rd)			X
Delay steal (bases loaded)			X
Delay steal (man on 3rd)			X
Hit and run play		X	
Fake steal		X	
Drag bunt (for base hit)		X	
Sacrifice bunt (move runner one base)		X	
Sacrifice bunt (move runner two bases)		X	
Safe-squeeze bunt		X	
Suicide squeeze (score one run)		X	
Suicide squeeze (score two runs)		X	
Fake bunt and slash (man on 1st or 2nd)		X	
Fake bunt and slash (man on 3rd)		X	
Fake bunt (man on 2nd)		X	
Fake bunt (man on 1st)		X	

Table 2.3 Baserunning Plays Broken Down by Types of Offensive Men Involved

Special situation	Name of play	Runners are alone	Batter is alone	Runner and batter cooperating
Before pitcher delivers	Double steal (men on 1st and 3rd)	X		
	Double steal (men on 1st and 3rd—2 outs)	X		
	Double steal (man on 3rd, batter walks—any number of outs)			X
While pitcher is delivering	Single steal (man on 1st)	X		
	Double steal (men on 1st and 2nd)	X		
	Triple steal (bases loaded)	X		
	Single steal (man on 3rd)	X		
	Double steal (men on 1st and 3rd)	X		
	Double steal (men on 1st and 3rd—2 outs)	X		
After the pitcher has delivered (catcher has the ball)	Double steal (men on 1st and 3rd)	X		
	Double steal (men on 1st and 3rd—2 outs)	X		
	Delay steal (man on 2nd)	X		
	Delay steal (men on 1st and 2nd)	X		
	Delay steal (men on 2nd and 3rd)	X		
	Delay steal (bases loaded)	X		
	Delay steal (man on 3rd)	X		
None	Hit and run			X
None	Fake steal	X		
Batter has intention of bunting	Drag bunt (for base hit)		X	X
	Sacrifice bunt (move runner one base)			X
	Sacrifice bunt (move runner two bases)			X
	Safe-squeeze bunt			X
	Suicide squeeze (score one run)			X
	Suicide squeeze (score two runs)			X
Fake bunts	Fake bunt and slash (man on 1st or 2nd)			X
	Fake bunt and slash (man on 3rd)			X
	Fake bunt (man on 2nd)			X
	Fake bunt (man on 1st)			X

The players chosen for these mathematical experiments were in every case runners of *average* speed. Conversely, in every case I chose catchers and infielders of *above-average* ability. If there is any bias in this study, it is entirely in favor of the defense. These findings are presented in Tables 2.4 and 2.5. Each of the possible 24 throws and each of the possible 17 runs was timed on 25 occasions before averaging. Although I gave every advantage to the defense, the runners always maintained an overall superiority.

Table 2.4 Timing of Throws Made Against Running Plays (in Seconds)

Play	Time (seconds)
3rd to 1st (ball bunted 30 ft from plate)	1.4
3rd to 1st (ball bunted 40 ft from plate)	1.3
3rd to 1st (bunt between pitcher and 3rd)	1.2
3rd to 1st	1.6
3rd to 2nd	1.2
3rd to home	1.2
Catcher to pitcher (lob)	1.0
Catcher to pitcher (fast)	0.8
Catcher to 2nd	1.75
Catcher to 3rd	1.3
Catcher to 1st	1.3
Catcher to 2nd, cutoff behind pitcher	1.3
Pitcher to batter at 70 mph	0.9
Pitcher to 1st or 2nd or 3rd	0.8
2nd or shortstop on 2nd to home	1.8
2nd or shortstop on 2nd to 1st	1.4
2nd or shortstop on 2nd to 3rd	1.3
1st to home	1.4
1st to 2nd	1.4
1st to 3rd	1.8
Lob rundown (20 ft apart)	1.0
Full hesitation (between a catch and a throw)	1.0
Half hesitation (between a catch and a throw)	0.5
Right field to 3rd (no cutoff)	2.8

Table 2.5 Times of Distances Run by Baserunners (in Seconds)

Play	Time (seconds)
Run to 1st	
For right-handed hitter	4.1
For left-handed hitter	3.9
Run 1st to 2nd	
10-ft lead off 1st	3.6
20-ft lead off 1st	3.2
30-ft lead off 1st	2.7
40-ft lead off 1st	2.3
Total run 1st to 2nd	4.1
Run 2nd to 3rd	
10-ft lead off 2nd	3.6
20-ft lead off 2nd	3.2
30-ft lead off 2nd	2.7
40-ft lead off 2nd	2.3
Total run 2nd to 3rd	4.1
Run 3rd to home	
10-ft lead off 3rd	3.6
20-ft lead off 3rd	3.2
30-ft lead off 3rd	2.7
40-ft lead off 3rd	2.3
Total run 3rd to home	4.1

Note. Any differences in a runner's ability to get the "jump" on the pitcher were averaged out when arriving at the figures in this table.

Explanation of the Times of Runners and Throwers

An objection to the validity of these surprising statistics might arise because I based them solely on high school and American Legion level performance. Yet at every level below those studied, it is well known that the runner is almost always ahead of the catcher and pitcher. In Colt, Pony, and all leagues below, the catcher's arm and pitcher's speed are slower than the runner due to the physical development of young players. In other words, the lower the level, the better these plays should work.

At every level above those studied, the runner will not be significantly ahead of the pitcher and catcher. In junior college, college, semipro, and professional ball, the arms of all infielders improve greatly over lower levels. But proportionately, the runner does not make the same gains. Ascending toward the top levels of the game, defensive players also become smarter and able to react better in unusual situations.

Of course, runners become faster, smarter, and more experienced, too. I have no idea how many of these baserunning plays would be consistently successful in the major leagues. No team in history has tried them all. Running and throwing times would certainly decrease with each step up the ladder. I believe, however, that the results would be nearly the same—runners should still have a slight advantage in most plays executed correctly by professionals.

In the following analysis of the individual plays, I have determined to the one tenth second the exact margin of difference between the runner's time and the total time for maneuvers by the defense. Sometimes wide, sometimes narrow, this fraction is usually in favor of the offense. Also a diagram accompanies each play, illustrating the components of the play. Let's look now at the details of the individual plays.

The 28 Plays

Play 1: Double Steal With Men on First and Third, None or One Out

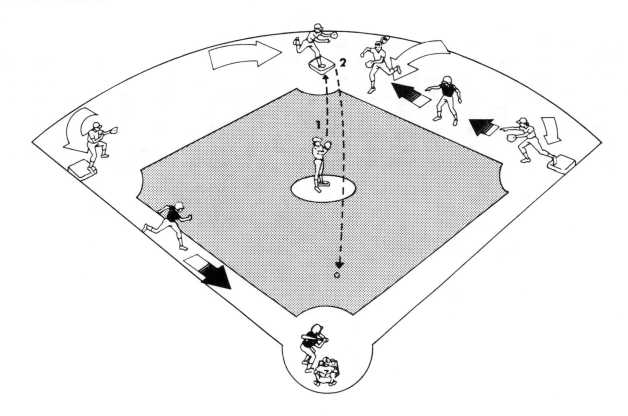

This play is designed to steal home and second base without giving up any outs. The psychological advantage is tremendous because the defense expects a steal play on or after the pitch—not before. Based totally on the element of surprise, the success rate is 80 percent or more.

Play Progression and Analysis

- Coach yells, "O.K.," then shouts last name of first-base runner, followed by the number of outs. Third-base runner and batter hear this sign.
- First-base runner waits until the pitcher is in the stretch. Just before the delivery, runner breaks hard toward second base. Everyone sitting on the bench yells, "Balk!"
- With none or one out, the runner keeps going hard and slides into second base; if ball is thrown to first, the runner gets into a trap.
- The instant the pitcher throws to the area around second base, the third-base runner breaks for the plate, sliding hard.
- As the throw goes home, the first-base runner then steals second.

Timing Analysis

Relay toss from second baseman to first baseman	= 1.00 seconds
First baseman's hesitation	= 1.00 seconds
First baseman's throw to home plate	= 1.40 seconds
Total time of all throws	= 3.40 seconds
Third-base runner's time to home plate	= 3.20 seconds

The runner on third base should beat the throw home by 0.2 of a second.

Defensing the Play

Because of the surprise element, this is extremely difficult to defense. To beat this, pitcher fakes a throw to second-base area, then fires to third base. The runner should be leaning off!

Helpful Tips

The runner on first base must be very casual and act out his part. The pitcher will probably be rubbing the ball on the mound and will have his guard down. The defense will not be set to work the first- and third-base cutoff plays. Be certain the third-base runner has the maximum lead when the break for home plate is begun. This play is so difficult to defense that if the opponent elects to tag the first-base runner, the run will score. The third-base runner must break just as the toss leaves the second baseman's hand to the first baseman. Or, the third-base runner can break the instant he sees the ball leave the pitcher's hand for the second-base area. To make this play most effective, mix it up with the other four first-base and third-base double steals, namely the before-the-pitch and after-the-pitch types of steals.

Play 2: Double Steal With Men on First Base and Third Base With Two Outs

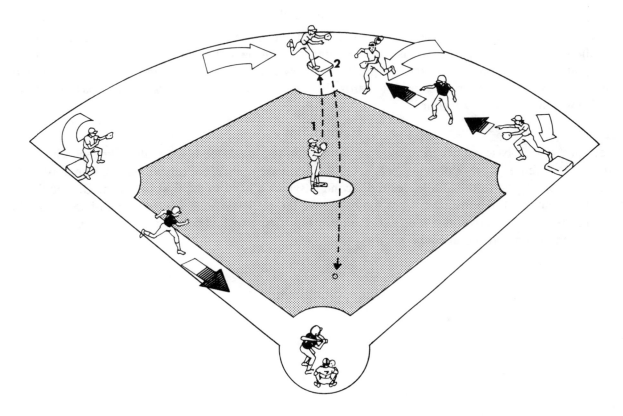

This play is designed to steal home and to steal second base without giving up any outs, but it may only score a run before the third out, ending the inning. As in Play 1, the psychological advantage is tremendous. The defense will not expect this attempt with two outs, nor will it expect this play before the pitch. The success rate for this play is at least 80 percent because it is based completely on the element of surprise.

Play Progression and Analysis

- Coach yells, "O.K.," then the last name of the first-base runner, followed by "two away."
- Third-base runner and batter hear the same sign.
- First-base runner waits until pitcher is coming down in the stretch. Just before the delivery, first-base runner breaks hard for second base, then suddenly stops halfway.
- Runner forces a rundown between first and second base. The third-base runner breaks for the plate at just the correct instant—the moment second baseman throws to first baseman.
- With two outs, be certain that the trapped runner does not allow himself to be tagged out until the third-base runner crosses the plate. Otherwise, the run does not count, and the inning is over.

Timing Analysis

Pitcher's throw to second-base area	= 0.80 seconds
Time of second baseman's toss to first baseman	= 1.00 seconds
First baseman's hesitation time	= 1.00 seconds
Time of throw from first baseman to catcher	= 1.40 seconds
Or from second baseman to catcher	= 1.75 seconds

> Combined times of all throws (first base to catcher) = 3.40 seconds
> (second base to catcher) = 3.75 seconds
> Time of runner from third base to home = 3.20 seconds

The third-base runner will reach home plate either 0.2 or 0.55 seconds ahead of the throw.

Defensing the Play

Pitcher should step off the rubber and run right at the man trapped between first and second. He should try to chase the runner back to first base, tag the runner, or throw out the third-base runner if he breaks for the plate. A second choice requires the pitcher to throw to the second baseman, who has charged into the baseline. He chases the runner back towards first. He also has a good view of third base and is in a good position for a throw to third.

Helpful Tips

Be certain the third-base runner has maximum lead when the break for home plate is begun. This play is difficult to defense. If the opponent elects to tag the first-base runner, the run will score. The third-base runner must break just as the toss leaves the second baseman's hand to the first baseman. Or, the third-base runner can break the instant he sees the ball leave the pitcher's hand for the second-base area. To make this play most effective, mix it up with the other four first-base and third-base double steals, namely the before-the-pitch and the after-the-pitch types of steals.

Play 3: Double Steal With Runner on Third After the Batter Has Walked to First Base

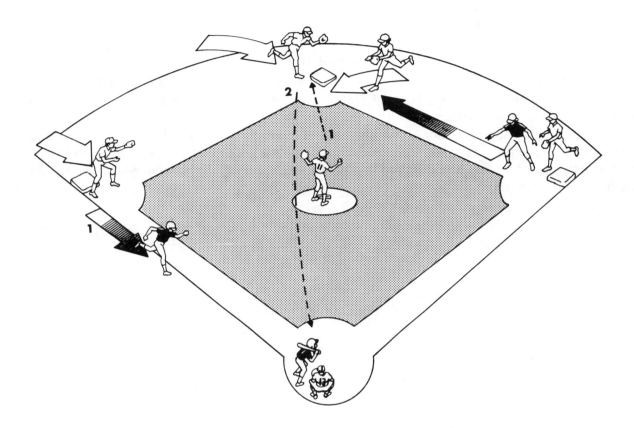

This unusual play is designed to steal home and steal second base without giving up any outs. The psychological advantage of the play is great; the defense is totally surprised because the play begins with the hitter walking to first base rather than being there earlier. This is one of the best running plays in baseball, with a success rate of 80 percent or better.

Play Progression and Analysis

- With a two- or three-ball count, call for a time-out and tell the batter, "If walked, jog to first base, stop on the bag, and wait for the pitcher to rub the ball or take his eyes off you. Be sure to act casual. Then break hard for second base."
- If there are no outs, instruct the player to slide into second base. If there are two outs, instruct player to stop halfway between second base and first base and get into a rundown.
- The runner on third base leads off slightly as the batter jogs to first base. Then, the third-base runner breaks for home plate when the pitcher actually throws to the shortstop or second baseman to tag the runner coming from first.

Timing Analysis

Pitcher's throw to second baseman	= 0.80 seconds
Hesitation time of second baseman	= 1.10 seconds
Time of throw from second baseman to catcher	= 1.80 seconds
Total time of throws	= 3.70 seconds
Time of runner on third base to home plate	= 3.60 seconds

The runner on third base should beat the throw home by 0.1 of a second.

Defensing the Play

This play also is quite difficult to defense. Pitcher should step off rubber and fire the ball to second baseman. The first and second basemen should run down the first-base runner, but fire home if third-base runner breaks for the plate.

Helpful Tips

Be sure the batter acts out his part, moving casually from home plate to first. Pitcher will be off or on the rubber, maybe rubbing the ball. His back will be to the play. Infielders are not in position to defense first and third bases, at that moment.

Third-base runner breaks for home plate the instant he sees the ball leave the pitcher's hand toward second base. Or, he may break and score on the rundown tosses. To make this play most effective, mix it up with the other four first-base and third-base double steals, namely the before-the-pitch and the after-the-pitch types of steals.

Play 4: Single Steal on the Pitcher

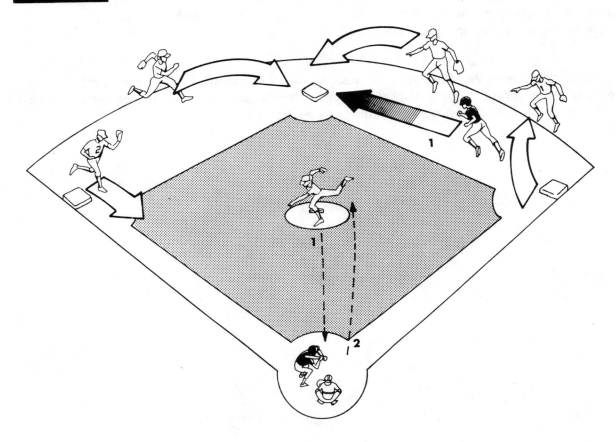

The purpose of this play is to steal a runner from first to second base with no help from the batter. There is no element of surprise because this play is anticipated by all defenses. If successful, the play creates some psychological advantage, for the runner moves into scoring position. A team, if stealing with its fastest men only, usually expects 50 percent success from this play.

Play Progression and Analysis

- Runner receives the steal-on-pitcher sign.
- Runner takes maximum lead, on each pitch, at all times.
- Runner must be sure pitcher has started to commit himself to the plate.
- Runner needs quick first step to get maximum acceleration. Slide hard.
- Runner should get up fast and be ready to advance on an overthrown ball.

Timing Analysis

Time of pitch	= 0.90 seconds
Time of catcher's hesitation before throw	= 0.30 seconds
Time of catcher's throw	= 1.75 seconds
Combined times of all above	= 2.95 seconds
First-base runner's time	= 3.20 seconds

The average runner should be thrown out at second base by 0.25 seconds.

Defensing the Play

- Be sure pitcher throws over to first base if runner takes too much lead.
- If catcher suspects a steal is on, call for a pitchout, an outside pitch.
- Make sure shortstop and second baseman know who will cover the catcher's throw.
- When runner breaks, all infielders should yell, "There he goes."

Helpful Tips

Be sure the runner receives the steal sign. Base coach should assist runner by having runner get off base far enough to get the proper jump on the pitcher. On this play, the successful base runner steals the base on the pitcher's motion, not on the catcher's throw to second base.

Play 5: Double Steal on the Pitcher

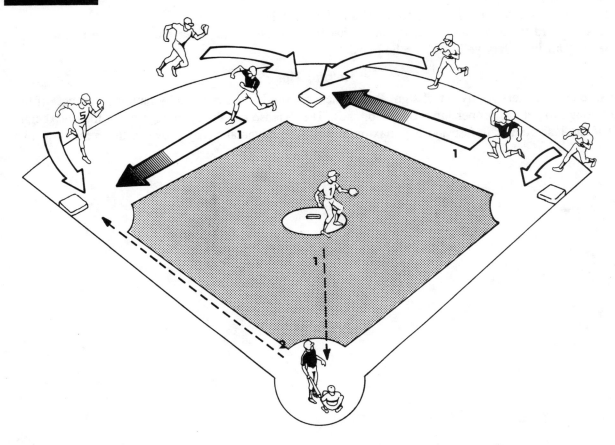

The purpose of this play is to steal men from first and second to second and third while pitcher delivers. The runners get no help from the batter. This tactic advances both runners into scoring position and removes possible double plays at second and first base. The success rate of this double steal is 50 percent with a fast lead runner.

Play Progression and Analysis

- Both runners get the steal sign from the coach.
- First- and second-base runners take maximum leads.
- Both runners must be sure pitcher has committed delivery to the plate.

Timing Analysis

Time of pitch	= 0.90 seconds
Time of catcher's hesitation before throw	= 0.40 seconds
Time of catcher's throw to third	= 1.30 seconds
Combined times of all above	= 2.60 seconds
Second-base runner's time	= 3.20 seconds
First-base runner's time	= 3.60 seconds

If the defense makes no miscues, then the ball should beat the runner to third base by 0.6 seconds.

Defensing the Play

- Never let a second-base runner have too much lead. Work your second-base pickoff throws to keep runner close.
- If catcher suspects a steal is on, catcher calls for a pitchout.
- Be sure third baseman doesn't creep in so that it is impossible to cover the base on a throw.
- Be sure all infielders yell, "There he goes."

Helpful Tips

Be sure both runners receive steal sign. Base coaches should assist runners by having them get off base far enough to get the proper jump on the pitcher. The defense has the advantage when the play begins, but if the lead runner is fast and has maximum lead, the advantage may move to the running team.

Play 6: Triple Steal on the Pitcher

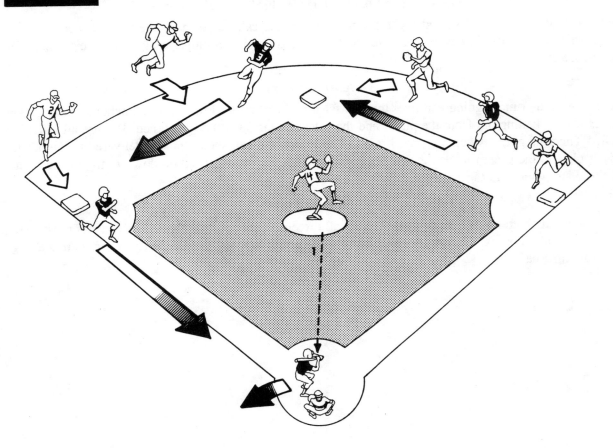

The purpose of this play is to steal three men to next bases, stealing home while the pitcher delivers. This is one of baseball's most difficult and daring running plays. Psychologically, to be the victim of a steal-home play on a triple steal is devastating to a team's morale. The success rate is, obviously, very low (10 percent). The lead runner must be incredibly swift, and all other necessary factors must be perfect, working together for the running team.

Play Progression and Analysis

- Man on third base is the key here. This runner must be extremely fast and get maximum jump on the pitcher.
- Pitcher must wind up and not take usual stretch.
- If pitcher takes the stretch, all runners know the play is off. This play will fail if pitcher is in the stretch.
- Runners on first and second bases take a big lead. Do not slide at next bases, but take big, wide turns, ready to steal another base if the ball gets away from the catcher.
- All runners make sure pitcher winds up before they go.
- All three runners must beware of pickoff plays. This is when the opponent will try them.
- Third-base runner should slide hard and low, away from pitcher's throw and tag by catcher.

Timing Analysis

Time of pitch	= 0.90 seconds
Time of catcher hesitation	= 0.50 seconds
Total of all above	= 1.40 seconds

Time of third-base runner's run   = 2.30 seconds
Time of first-base runner to second = 3.20 seconds
Time of second-base runner to third = 3.20 seconds

We conclude that the ball should reach the position for the catcher to make the tag 0.9 seconds ahead of the sliding runner. However, this assumes that defense makes no miscue against the extremely fast third-base runner.

Defensing the Play

Pitcher sees the runner going and fires the ball far inside and rather low to assist catcher in the tag. The batter will be bailing out from the pitch, and the catcher's tag should be easy then. Be sure all infielders yell, "There he goes" when a runner breaks. The reason the ball should not be delivered to the outside of the plate is the time it takes the catcher to move from the outside position down to the inside corner of the plate where the tag is made.

Helpful Tips

Be very certain batter gets take sign. Be certain all three runners get steal sign. Base coaches must watch for pickoffs at all bases. Third-base coach should be certain to assist third-base runner in getting a huge lead off third base.

Play 7: Single Steal Home on Pitcher

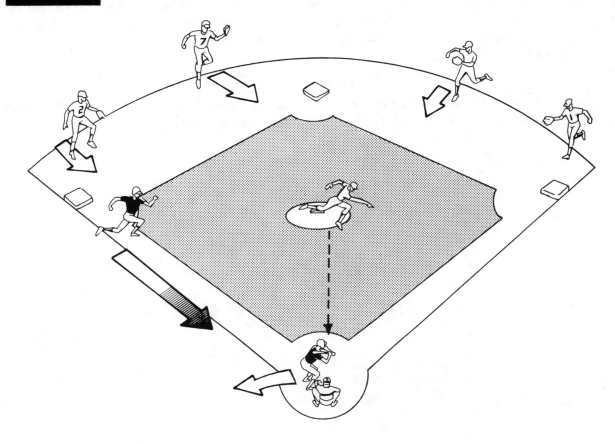

The purpose of this play is to steal home and score a run while the pitcher is in the windup—thus performing one of baseball's most difficult and daring running plays. Psychologically, to be the victim of a steal-home play is devastating to a team's morale. The success rate is obviously low (10 percent). The runner must be incredibly swift, and all other factors must be perfectly together for the running team.

Play Progression and Analysis

- Man is on third base with no other runners on the bases.
- Runner must be extremely fast and get a maximum jump on the pitcher.
- Pitcher must wind up, not taking his stretch.
- If pitcher takes his stretch, runner knows the play is off. This play will fail if the pitcher is in his stretch.
- Third-base runner makes sure pitcher has started the motion and is committed to the plate.
- Runner must beware of a pickoff play.
- Runner should slide hard and low in a hook slide away from the pitcher's throw and tag by the catcher.

Timing Analysis

Time of pitch	= 0.90 seconds
Time of catcher's hesitation	= 0.50 seconds
Total of all above	= 1.40 seconds
Time of third-base runner's run	= 2.30 seconds

If the defense makes no miscues, then the ball will beat the runner to home plate by 0.9 seconds. However, this assumes the defense makes no miscues against the extremely fast third-base runner.

Defensing the Play

The pitcher sees the runner going and fires the ball far inside and rather low to assist catcher in the tag. The batter will be bailing out from the pitch, and the catcher's tag should be easy then. Be sure all infielders yell, "There he goes" when runner breaks. The reason the ball should not be delivered outside the plate is the extra time it takes the catcher to move from the outside position down to the inside corner of the plate where the tag is made.

Helpful Tips

Be certain the batter gets take sign and the runner sees the steal sign. Third-base coach should be alert for pickoff play and assist third-base runner in getting huge lead off base.

Play 8: Double Steal on the Pitcher With Men on First and Third With None or One Out

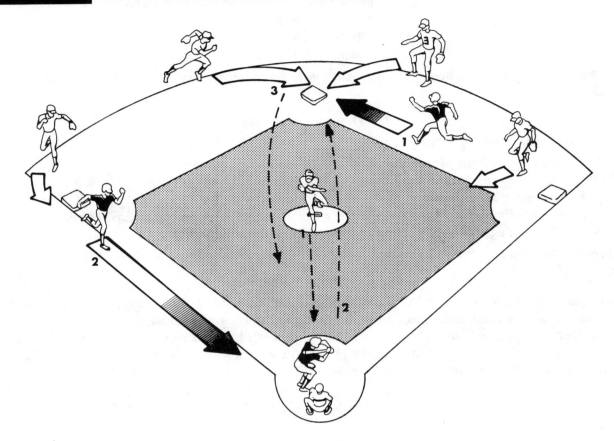

The purpose of this play is to steal home and second base and have no one put out. The psychological advantage of this play is not too great, because this is one play that all defenses spend a great deal of time practicing. Even though it is difficult to defense, the defense is ready for it, so the element of surprise is lacking. Surprisingly, though, if used sparingly, this play should still give the running team a 70 percent rate of success.

Play Progression and Analysis

- Coach gives steal sign to first-base runner. Coach indicates to third-base runner that a double-steal play is on.
- First-base runner steals on the pitch.
- Third-base runner edges off as pitcher delivers. Runner must have a good lead.
- Catcher now has the ball. Catcher fires to second base to infielder covering the base.
- The instant the third-base runner sees the ball go past the pitcher on the mound, runner breaks for the plate and slides.
- As the runner going to second base sees the throw going back to the plate, runner steals second base, sliding.
- Only your fastest runners will be able to make it from third base to home on this play against good catcher and infield arms.

Timing Analysis

Time of pitch to the plate	= 0.90 seconds
Time of catcher's throw to second base	= 1.75 seconds
Time of second-base throw back to the plate	= 1.75 seconds
Total time of the path of the ball	= 4.40 seconds
Time of third-base runner's run to the plate	= 3.20 seconds

If the defense makes no miscues (and no hesitations), the runner will still beat the ball to home plate by 0.3 of a second.

Defensing the Play

The five infield-cutoff options:

- Second baseman cuts off the throw.
- Catcher fakes and fires to third base.
- Pitcher cuts off the throw.
- Pitcher lets the throw go through. Tag is made at second, and the ball is fired home.
- Player covering second has option of cutting off or throwing through.

Practice these options every day against men on first base and third base steals.

Helpful Tips

Be certain the first-base runner has a good lead and that the first-base runner gets a good jump on the pitcher. Warn the third-base runner about the five cutoff options the defense can use.

Runner must be certain the ball travels beyond the pitcher's head when catcher throws to second base. The break for home must be at that moment, from a maximum lead. To make this play most effective, mix it up with the other four first-base and third-base double steals.

Play 9: Double Steal on the Pitcher With Men on First and Third and Two Outs

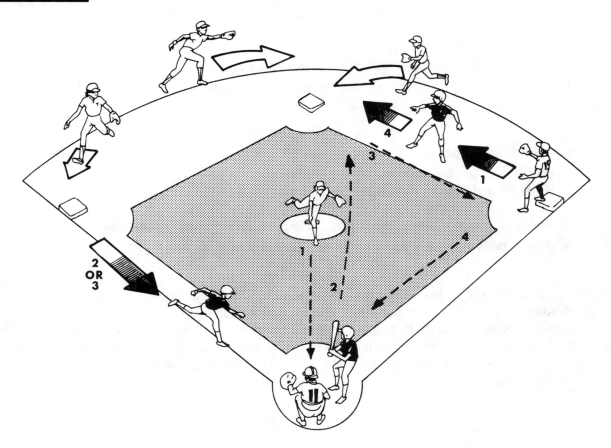

The purpose of this play is to score a run from a steal home and to steal second with no one put out. If the third out is made on the second-base play, the runner must cross home plate first. The psychological advantage of this play is not too great because this is another play that all defenses spend a great deal of time practicing. Even though it is difficult to defense, the defense is set for it, so the element of surprise is lacking. Surprisingly, though, if used sparingly, this play should still give the running team a 70 percent rate of success.

Play Progression and Analysis

- Coach gives steal sign to first-base runner. Coach also yells the number of outs: "Two." Coach indicates to the third-base runner that a double steal is on.
- First-base runner steals on the pitch.
- Third-base runner edges off as the pitcher delivers. Runner must have a good lead.
- Catcher has the ball and fires to second-base area, but the first-base runner stops halfway to second base. Now a rundown starts on the first-base runner.
- The instant the third-base runner sees the ball sail beyond the pitcher, runner breaks for the plate and slides. Then there will be no trap play between first and second.
- As the trapped first-base runner sees the ball thrown to the plate, runner proceeds to steal second base. Trapped runner must not be tagged out before the run scores.
- Only the fastest runners can make it from third base to home.

Timing Analysis

Time of pitch to the plate	= 0.90 seconds
Time of catcher's throw to second base	= 1.75 seconds
Lob throw (if a trap play ensues later)	= 1.00 seconds
First-base throw home	= 1.40 seconds
Total time of the path of the ball	= 3.50 seconds
Time of third-base runner's run to the plate	= 3.20 seconds

If the defense makes no miscues (and makes no hesitations), then the runner will beat the ball to the plate by 0.3 of a second.

Defensing the Play

The four infield-cutoff options:

- Second baseman or shortstop cuts off the throw.
- Catcher fakes and fires to third base.
- Pitcher cuts off the throw.
- Pitcher lets throw go through, tag is made at second, and the ball is fired home.

Practice these options every day against men on first and third base steals.

Helpful Tips

Be certain first-base runner has a good lead. Be certain first-base runner gets good jump on the pitcher. Warn third-base runner about the five cutoff options defense can use.

The runner must be certain the ball travels beyond the pitcher's head when the catcher throws to second base. His break for home must be at that moment from a maximum lead. To make this play most effective, mix it up with the other four first-base and third-base double steals, namely the before-the-pitch and the after-the-pitch types of steals.

Play 10: Double Steal on the Catcher's Throw Back to the Pitcher, None or One Out, With Runners on First and Third Bases

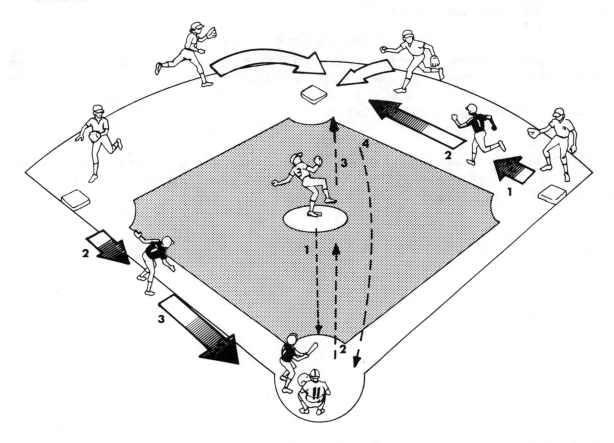

The purpose of this play is to steal home and second base with no one put out. The psychological advantage of this play is very great. Opponents do not expect a steal play after the catcher receives the ball. Success rate of this play is very high (75 percent).

Play Progression and Analysis

- No verbal sign is given. Coach gives delay-steal sign. This play is a form of delayed steal.
- First-base runner leads off a normal amount and comes back only one half a step.
- Be sure first-base runner does not lean toward second base. This will give the play away.
- The instant the first-base runner sees the ball leave the catcher's hand to return to the pitcher, runner takes off in a sprint. If none or one are out, keep going and slide.
- Third-base runner takes a lead as the pitcher receives the catcher's return toss.
- The instant the third-base runner sees the ball leave pitcher's hand for second-base area, runner breaks for the plate and slides.
- First-base runner steals second on the throw to home plate.

Timing Analysis

Time of catcher's toss back to pitcher	= 0.80 seconds
Pitcher's hesitation time on the mound area	= 0.30 seconds
Pitcher's quick throw to second-base area	= 0.80 seconds
Second base hesitation	= 0.60 seconds
Second base throw back to the plate	= 1.80 seconds

| Total of all the above paths of ball | = 3.50 seconds |
| Time of third-base runner's run | = 3.30 seconds |

If the defense makes no miscues, then the third-base runner (who is 20 feet off third base) will arrive at the plate 0.2 seconds ahead of the ball.

Defensing the Play

Since it is a surprise play, surprise the runners. As soon as the pitcher receives the ball from the catcher and realizes that the first-base runner is stealing, pitcher fakes a hard throw to second base, then fires to third and picks off the third-base runner. The third-base runner should be trapped between home and third. Chase the runner back to third, not to home.

Helpful Tips

Be certain the third-base runner has a good lead. This is an extremely difficult play to defense. Be sure first-base runner takes normal lead on the pitch and moves back toward first base slightly. Do not lean toward second base. Both runners must be good actors.

Play 11: Double Steal on the Catcher's Throw Back to the Pitcher, Two Outs, With Runners on First and Third Bases

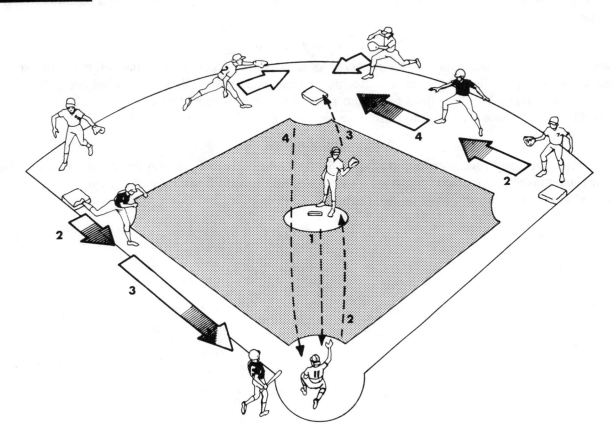

The purpose of this play is to steal home and steal second base with no one put out. The psychological advantage is very great. Opponents do not expect a steal play after the catcher receives the ball. Success rate of this play is very high (75 percent).

Play Progression and Analysis

- No verbal sign is given. Coach gives delay-steal sign. This play is a form of delayed steal.
- First-base runner leads off a normal amount and comes back only one-half step.
- Be sure first-base runner does not lean toward second base. This will give the play away.
- The instant the first-base runner sees the ball leave the catcher's hand to return to pitcher, runner takes off in a sprint. Runner suddenly stops halfway to second base.
- Third-base runner leads off as the pitcher gets the return toss.
- The instant the third-base runner sees the ball leave the pitcher's hand for the second-base area, runner breaks for the plate and slides.
- First-base runner steals second on the throw to home plate.

Timing Analysis

Time of catcher's toss back to pitcher	= 0.80 seconds
Pitcher's hesitation time on the mound area	= 0.30 seconds
Pitcher's quick throw to second-base area	= 0.80 seconds
Second base hesitation	= 0.60 seconds
Second base throw back to the plate	= 1.80 seconds

Total of all of the above paths of the ball   = 3.50 seconds
Time of third-base runner's run   = 3.30 seconds

If the defense makes no miscues, then the third-base runner (who is 20 feet off third base) will arrive at the plate 0.2 seconds ahead of the ball.

Defensing the Play

Since it is a surprise play, surprise the runners. As soon as the pitcher receives the ball from the catcher and realizes that the first-base runner is stealing, pitcher fakes a hard throw to second base, then fires to third base and picks off the third-base runner. The third-base runner should be trapped between home and third base. Chase him back to third base, not to home.

Helpful Tips

Be certain third-base runner has a good lead. This is an extremely difficult play to defense. Be sure first-base runner takes a normal lead on the pitch and moves back toward first base slightly. Do not lean toward second base. Both runners must be good actors.

Play 12: Delayed Steal on the Catcher's Throw to Second Base With Runner on Second Base

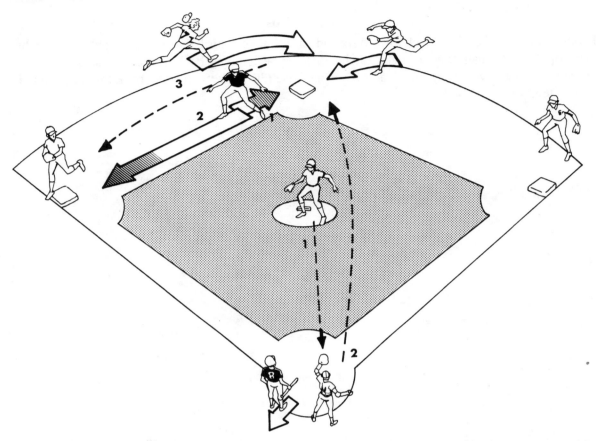

The purpose of this play is to steal third base by fooling the catcher, drawing his throw to second base. Any delayed-steal play has a great psychological advantage because the timing of the play is different from what the defense expects. The success rate for this steal is 30 percent, unless the second-base runner is extremely swift.

Play Progression and Analysis

- Runner on second base receives delay-steal sign from the coach.
- As the pitch is made, second-base runner dashes off second base about 30-35 feet.
- Runner acts as if to head back to second base.
- If the catcher fires a pickoff throw to second base, the runner breaks for third base. Runner slides hard.
- Runner actually is beating two throws (from catcher to second base and from second to third base).

Timing Analysis

Time of catcher's throw to second base	= 1.75 seconds
Hesitation by the infielder taking the throw	= 0.50 seconds
Time of throw from second base to third base	= 1.30 seconds
Total of all the above	= 3.55 seconds
Time of second-base runner's run to third base	= 3.30 seconds

If the defense makes no miscues, then the runner will beat the ball to third base by 0.25 seconds.

Defensing the Play

The catcher fires ball back to the pitcher. The pitcher then runs at the second-base runner and traps him off the base, then a rundown occurs.

Helpful Tips

Tell your runner to fake a lean back toward second base, but keep his balance and weight so he can break quickly for third. Runner tries to make catcher believe he is going back to second base.

The runner must have a very long lead off second base (30-35 feet) and lean back toward second base only one step.

Play 13: Delayed Steal on the Catcher's Throw to First Base With Runners on First and Second Bases

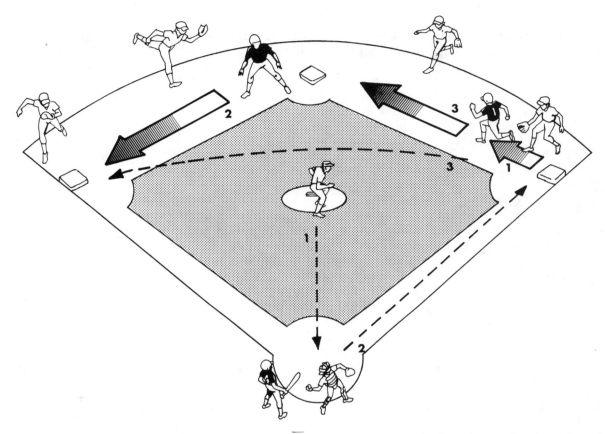

The purpose of this play is to double-steal second and third bases by fooling the catcher into throwing to first base. The success rate for this particular delayed steal is quite high, 50 percent, or much higher if the second-base runner is extremely swift.

Play Progression and Analysis

- Both runners on first and second bases get delayed-steal sign from coach.
- Man on first base breaks off the base about 35 feet. Man on second base edges off the base a maximum lead, around 20-25 feet.
- Suddenly, catcher fires a pickoff throw to first base. Runner is now trapped off base.
- Just as the ball leaves the catcher's hand, the second-base runner goes to third base, sliding hard.
- First baseman will throw too late to third base to get the runner there.
- As the ball leaves first baseman's hand, first-base runner steals to second base.

Timing Analysis

Time of catcher's throw to first base	= 1.30 seconds
First baseman's hesitation time	= 0.50 seconds
Time of first baseman's throw to third base	= 1.80 seconds
Total of all of the above	= 3.60 seconds
Time of second-base runner's run to third base	= 3.20 seconds

If the defense makes no miscues, then the second-base runner will arrive at third base 0.4 seconds before the ball.

Defensing the Play

Catcher fires ball back to the pitcher. The pitcher runs at the runner off first base, and runs him back to first base. The runner on second base won't dare break for third base.

Helpful Tips

Be sure first-base runner takes a far lead off first base and acts as if to try to get back to first. Be sure second-base runner has enough lead to get to third base, but not enough to draw catcher's throw.

Play 14: Delayed Steal on the Catcher's Throw to Second Base With Runners on Second and Third Bases

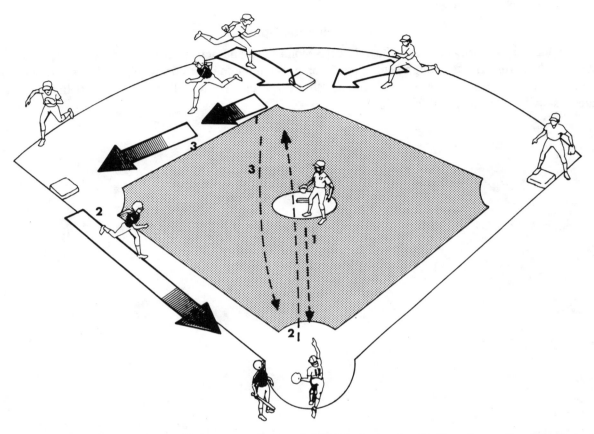

The purpose of this play is to double-steal two bases, including home, by fooling the catcher into throwing to second base with a runner on third base. Success rate on this play for stealing both bases, including home, is 40 percent.

Play Progression and Analysis

- Runners on second base and third base get delayed-steal sign from coach.
- Man off second base breaks 35 feet toward third base on the pitch. Man on third base edges slowly off third on the pitch.
- Catcher fires a pickoff throw to second base. As the ball leaves the catcher's hand, man on third base breaks hard for the plate, slides hard.
- Second baseman fires home to throw out the runner at the plate.
- As second baseman releases the ball for home plate, the second-base runner steals third base easily.

Timing Analysis

Time of catcher's throw to second base	= 1.75 seconds
Hesitation time for second baseman	= 0.50 seconds
Time of second baseman's throw back to home	= 1.80 seconds
Total of all of the above	= 4.05 seconds
Time of third-base runner's run to home	= 3.60 seconds

If the defense makes no miscues, then the third-base runner (who is 10 feet off third) will arrive at the plate 0.45 seconds ahead of the ball.

Defensing the Play

The best way to defense this play is to have your catcher fire the ball back to the pitcher. Pitcher runs at runner off second base and runs him back to second and tags him. Third-base runner won't dare break for home during the rundown.

Helpful Tips

Be sure second-base runner breaks 35 feet off second base and acts as if returning to second base. Be sure third-base runner has enough lead to steal home, but not enough to draw the catcher's throw to third base. This play is a good sucker play for the ''hot dog'' catcher who likes to show off his great arm. Catchers will often fall for this tactic.

Play 15: Delayed Steal on the Catcher's Throw to First Base or Second Base With Bases Loaded

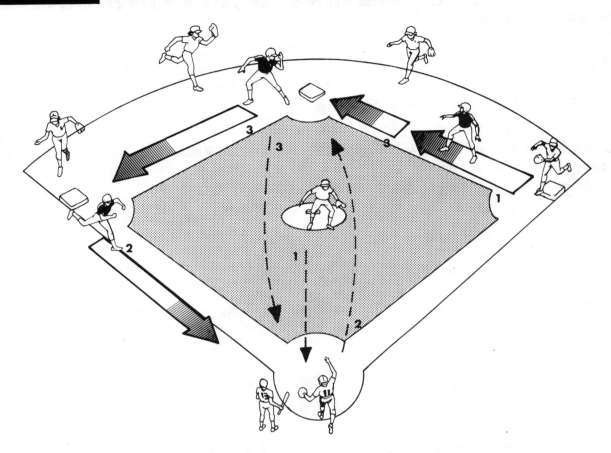

The purpose of this play is to steal three bases, including home, by fooling the catcher into throwing down to first base or the second-base area. No play in baseball offers your running team more of a psychological advantage than this one. It is so unusual, so untimely, that you have the element of complete surprise in your favor. Success rate is very high, around 75 percent for stealing all three bases, including home, without giving up even one out.

Play Progression and Analysis

- All three base runners receive delayed-steal sign from their coach.
- As the pitcher delivers, first-base runner breaks for second base, as if runner forgets a man occupies that base. He stops 20 feet from second base and looks startled. The batter has been given the "take" sign.
- Second-base runner stands on second base and yells loudly, "Get back," to the first-base runner.
- Third-base runner edges off his base cautiously, watching the scene.
- Catcher throws ball down to the second-base area. As the catcher releases the ball, the third-base runner breaks for home and beats the throw home from the second baseman. As the throw goes home, the other two base runners steal their next bases easily.

Timing Analysis

Time of catcher's throw to second base	= 1.75 seconds
Time of hesitation by the second baseman	= 0.50 seconds
Time of throw by second baseman back to home	= 1.80 seconds

Total of all of the above	= 4.05 seconds
Time of third-base runner's run to home	= 3.60 seconds

If the defense makes no miscues, then the third-base runner (who is 15 feet off third base) will arrive home 0.4 seconds ahead of the ball.

Defensing the Play

The best way to defense this play is to have the catcher tell the pitcher to cover the plate. Catcher runs out on diamond and runs the first-base runner into second base. Tag both men on second base. Fire home if the man breaks from third base.

Helpful Tips

Be certain that first- and second-base runners carry out their act. Both of them must look startled and create a lot of noise. The third-base runner must have a good lead off his base, but not get picked off. He must be off base at least 15 feet at the time the catcher throws the ball down.

Play 16: Delayed Steal on the Catcher's Throw to Third Base With a Runner on Third Base

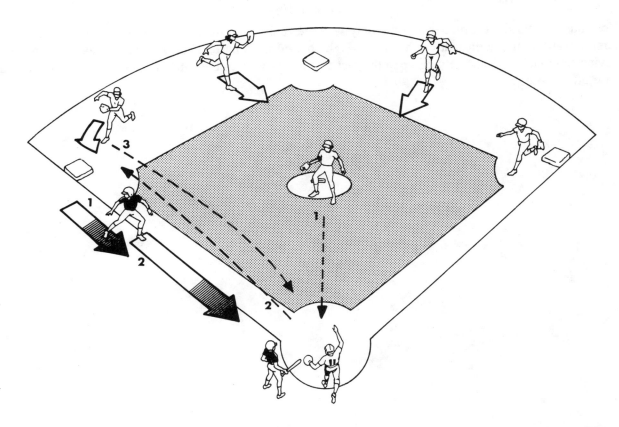

The purpose of this play is to steal home by fooling the catcher into throwing down to third base. Success rate on this play, unless the runner is extremely quick and fast, will be only 20 percent.

Play Progression and Analysis

- Man on third base gets delayed-steal sign from the coach.
- As the pitcher delivers, third-base runner yells, makes a lot of noise, and leans toward home, 35 feet off the base. Runner then fakes a lean back to third base.
- Catcher fires ball to third base; he thinks he has the runner picked off because the runner appears to be heading back in a dive to the base.
- The instant the third-base runner sees the ball leave the catcher's hands, runner breaks for the plate.
- Runner then beats the throw from third baseman back to the catcher.

Timing Analysis

Time of catcher's throw to third base	= 1.30 seconds
Third baseman's hesitation	= 0.50 seconds
Third baseman's throw to home	= 1.20 seconds
Total of all of the above	= 3.00 seconds
Time of third-base runner's run to home	= 2.70 seconds

If defense makes no miscues, the third-base runner (who is 30 feet off third base) will arrive at the plate about 0.3 seconds ahead of the ball.

Defensing the Play

The best way to defense this play is simple; the catcher walks out toward third base and fires to third for a pickoff just as the runner starts to dive back.

Helpful Tips

You must tell third-base runner that the only way the runner can make this play work is to get a quick jump toward home the instant catcher releases the ball to third base. The runner must take a chance by having too much lead and relying upon the fact that he knows that the catcher is going to throw to third base after the pitch.

Play 17: Hit and Run

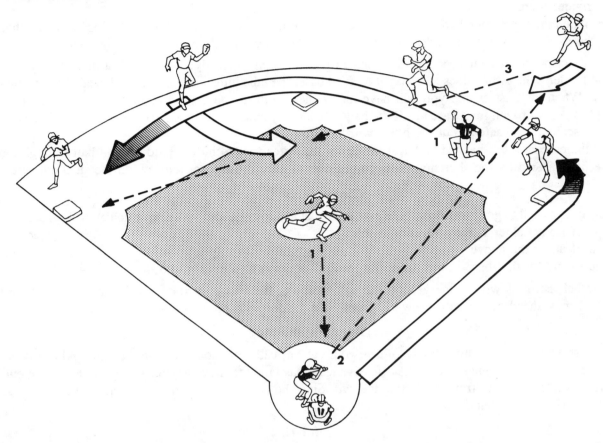

The purpose of this standard play is to move a runner up one or two bases, with the runner going and the batter swinging. Ideally, the ball will be hit through the hole vacated by the second baseman; the runners will end up at third and second bases at the completion of the play. This maneuver is rated as a "risk play." It can be worked with one runner on first, runners at first and second, or runners at first and third. When runners are on first and third, a separate signal must be given to the third-base runner indicating that he is not a part of the play. This play, correctly executed, may advance two runners a total of four bases and leave the defense no force plays at any bases, with first base left open. Success rate will be 50 percent, with the advance runner moved up one base, whether or not the batter will be out.

Play Progression and Analysis

- Men on base get the steal-on-pitcher sign from the coach.
- Batter gets a separate hit-and-run sign from the coach.
- We assume a right-handed batter at the plate. This is the only play in baseball where the batter must swing at the pitch, even if it is a bad one.
- Runners break with the pitcher, and steal the next bases.
- Hitter must swing at the pitch. If it is a terrible pitch, he merely fans the air with the bat, but does not hit the ball.
- Hitter tries to hit the ball on the ground through the hole vacated by shortstop or second baseman. Ideally, the hitter may hit a slicing low fly ball landing near the right field line.
- Runner on first base rounds second base and watches third-base coach's sign. Runner usually slides into third base.

- As the first-base runner steals, the second baseman covers second base to take the throw from the catcher.
- Hitter goes to second base, if possible, on the throw to third base from the outfield.
- The right fielder will have to play the hit ball. He will throw to third base in an attempt to get the runner there.
- When the hitter rounds first base and sees the ball thrown all the way through to third base, he then heads for second base, slides, and beats the third baseman's throw back to second base.

This description, of course, shows the planned play working perfectly. But if the cutoff man takes the right fielder's throw and does not relay it to third base, then the hitter rounds first and heads back to first base. When the dust clears, you will have men either on third and second or on third and first, if the ball has gone through for a base hit. If the ball is fielded by an infielder, the first-base runner will usually get to second base safely, but the hitter will be thrown out.

In the case of a left-handed batter at the plate, the hitter tries to hit the hard ground ball through the hole just vacated by the shortstop, who comes over to take the catcher's throw on the steal attempt.

Timing Analysis

Time it takes ball to go from pitcher's release to the bat and to be picked up by right fielder = 4.60 seconds
Time of right fielder's throw to third base = 2.80 seconds
Total of all of the above = 7.40 seconds
Time of run by first-base runner from the lead-off position to the slide into third base = 6.80 seconds

If the ball is hit slowly on the ground through the hole, the first-base runner will arrive at third base 0.6 seconds ahead of the ball thrown in from right fielder with no cut or relay.

Defensing the Play

The best way to defense this play is to have your catcher call a pitchout, receive the ball, and throw out the most advancing runner. Now, the offensive team has failed to move anyone along and loses one out. This prevents the batter from contacting the ball. Since he is forced to swing at the ball on the play, you have a strike on the batter, too.

Helpful Tips

Be certain that both the runners and the batter get both signs and that the first-base runner gets a big lead so he can make it to third base. Be sure the hitter goes to second base, if the throw goes through. Most importantly, the batter must swing at any pitch which he can get his bat on. He is protecting the runner.

Advantages of Hit-and-Run Play

- If successful, you will advance two runners a maximum of four bases and allow the batter an easy base hit.
- You open up gaping holes for an easier hit.
- You take the force play away from the defense, for now first base will be unoccupied when the next batter steps up.
- Most importantly, you now have two men in scoring position for the next batter to drive in.
- You outfoxed the defense, giving your team a psychological advantage.
- You can call this play with nearly any count or any number of outs.
- You prevent the double play against you. If the infield fields the ground ball, it has only a play at first base.
- If you are thrown out at first, you have just one man advanced into scoring position.
- If batter misses the pitch, his bat is a visual hazard to the catcher, who is trying to throw out the stealing runner.
- If the hitter fails to make contact, you are stealing a man into scoring position without giving up the hitter's out.

Disadvantages of the Hit-and-Run Play

- If the batter hits a deep or medium fly, first-base runner has to hustle back to first base, or he will be doubled up.
- If the ball is lined directly at an infielder, he will throw to first base, and the runner will always be doubled up.
- Hitters who pull the ball have trouble batting late through opposite side holes.
- Sometimes the batter forgets he must swing, thus ruining the play and offering no visual hazard to the catcher.
- This play requires daily practice and players must want to execute it.
- Players must learn to move their feet and arms in the batter's box to hit late. Their normal swing must be altered so that they "spank" the ball, letting up on their swing.
- Players have trouble getting the ball on the ground. When they swing late, they tend to hit the ball on the fly.
- Batter must hope for an outside corner pitch. Such a pitch will greatly aid in his attempt to hit late.
- If the pitch is inside or to the middle of the plate, batter simply must hit it where it's pitched.

This is the premium baserunning play in baseball. You will have higher returns with it for the time spent than with any other single play. It must be practiced every day in batting practice.

Play 18: The Fake Steal

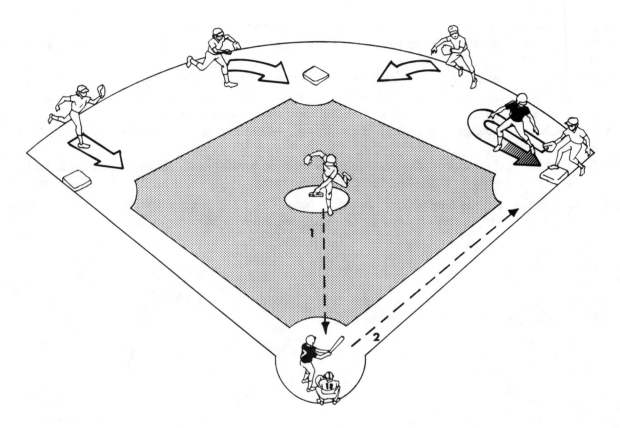

The purpose of this play is to set up the real steal play and/or to cause a bad pickoff throw at that base by the catcher. After this play has been used, the defense won't be able to distinguish a real steal from the fake steals. Great psychological damage can be done with this tactic. It worries the pitcher and catcher on every pitch, and the defense has to shade over, opening up defensive holes when a steal is bluffed by the running team. The success rate on this play is 100 percent, for no runner showing just a bluff or a fake steal should ever be picked off even by the best catcher's throw to a base.

Play Progression and Analysis

- Runner on base receives a fake-steal sign from the coach.
- Runner takes the lead, always leads off the maximum amount each time, and always leads off the same distance.
- As pitcher delivers, runner breaks down two steps hard and returns fast to base, ahead of the pickoff throw.
- All the defense will yell, "There he goes," on each fake-steal maneuver.
- Catcher will usually fire a pickoff throw to the runner's base.
- Runner must judge distance so that he gets maximum distance toward the next base in case of a hit ball and still prevents a pickoff from catcher's throw.

Timing Analysis

There is no mathematical analysis for a play of this type. Just remind each runner on your team who tries a fake steal to know exactly how much lead he can take and still be able to dive back safely on a pickoff throw. It will vary from runner to runner.

Defensing the Play

The best way to defense this play is to use pitcher and catcher pickoffs often. Hold the runner closer to the bag. Actually, there really is no way to prevent another team from doing this to you, but constant pitcher and catcher pickoff attempts can minimize the running team's efforts. Counter fake steals by keeping runners close to the bases and on guard.

Helpful Tips

Tell your runners to dart off and back, yelling, "Hey, pitcher!" Make a lot of noise, create a distraction. All runners should take maximum leads at all times. The more noise the runner makes and the more commotion created at the base area, the more effective the fake-steal attempt will be.

Play 19: Drag Bunt for a Hit

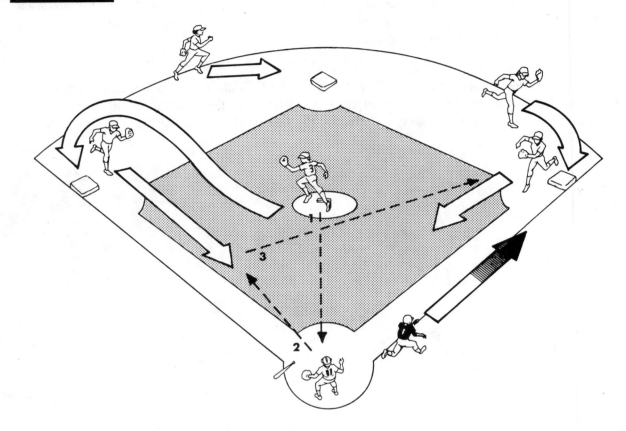

The purpose of this play is for the batter to lay down a perfect, slow-rolling bunt anywhere in fair territory, then beat the throw to first base. If the bunter performs this maneuver batting left-handed, he has the jump of a step or a step and one-half toward first base. The psychological advantage is great. Execute this play when the defense isn't expecting it. A success rate of 30 percent is good for drag bunting.

Play Progression and Analysis

- Batter gets the sign from the coach.
- If batter is right-handed, drag ball slowly to third baseman or first baseman.
- If batter is left-handed, drag ball slowly to third baseman.
- In either case, at the time of contact with the ball, batter must get a good jump toward first base.
- Batter has to run at top speed. It is always a close play.
- Batter should bunt only if the pitch is good.
- Be sure batter does not square around and show the bunt too soon. He wants to keep the infielders away from the plate.

Timing Analysis

Time of ball from contact on bat until it is picked up by third baseman	= 2.70 seconds
Time of throw to first base by the third baseman	= 1.40 seconds
Total of all of the above	= 4.10 seconds
Time of drag bunter's run from home to first	= 4.10 seconds

A very close play! If the defense makes no miscues and the third baseman has a good arm, then the bunter will arrive at first at the same time as the ball does. A tie always goes to the runner.

Defensing the Play

The best way to defense this play is always to have first baseman and third baseman play in a few steps until batter gets one strike on him. Best defense is a pair of fast first and third basemen with good arms. Pitcher must also stay alert and be able to get to the ball after the pitch is made. Only the pitcher, catcher, third baseman, and first baseman are involved in this play. Keep them very alert.

Helpful Tips

The whole concept of the drag bunt is based on the element of surprise. It can be tried with any number of outs and with any count on the batter. It surprises and exploits weak infielders.

Play 20: Sacrifice Bunt That Moves Runners One Base

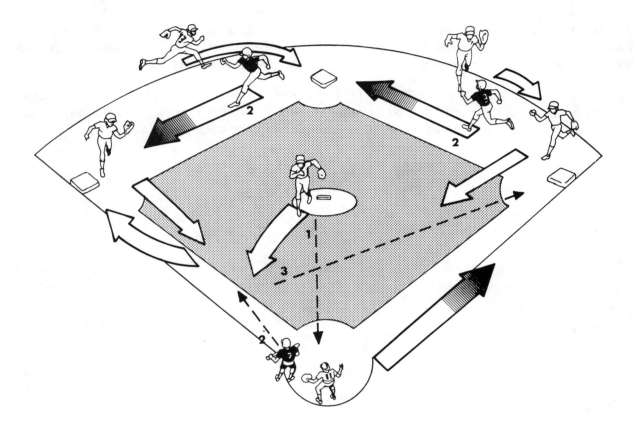

The purpose of this play is to move runners from first to second base or from second to third. We are willing to give up an out to do this. This tactic may also put two runners in scoring position and take double-play chances off at third base and second base.

The psychological advantage is not great on this play. Every team does it, expects it, and practices it. Success rate on sacrifice bunts should be 75 percent.

Play Progression and Analysis

- Batter and runner must both get the sacrifice-bunt sign from the coach.
- Runners may or may not be given the steal sign by the coach.
- If steal is given, hustle to next base and slide, whether bunt is a success or not, unless ball is popped up.
- If steal is not given, runner must be able to get to next base after the bunt is down. Runner must also be able to get back to the base if the bunt is missed.
- Usually the batter should bunt only strikes or close pitches.
- When executing a sacrifice bunt, batter should make his moves early enough to get bat out and make a good bunt.

Timing Analysis

Time of ball from contact on bat until infielder fields the ball = 2.50 seconds
Time of fielder's throw to first base = 1.30 seconds
Time of first-base runner's run to second base = 3.60 seconds
Time of bunter's run from home to first base = 4.10 seconds

If the defense makes no miscues, the first-base runner will beat a throw to second base by 0.2 seconds, but the bunter will arrive at first base 0.3 seconds behind the ball. Of course, time will vary with the placement and velocity of the bunt.

Defensing the Play

The best way to defense this play is to practice bunt shifts as a team, so that all six infielders are at the right spot. There is no real defense for this, if batter is a good bunter. Catcher can call for a pitchout if he suspects a sacrifice bunt on that pitch. That is not good defense, however, since the batter will bunt only a strike.

Helpful Tips

The play works if you can advance the men to their next bases. If bunter bunts too hard, the advancing runner will be forced out. Also, runners being advanced must have good leads. Emphasize to the batter that he is trying only to bunt softly, to get the ball on the ground somewhere.

Play 21: Sacrifice Bunt That Moves Runners Two Bases

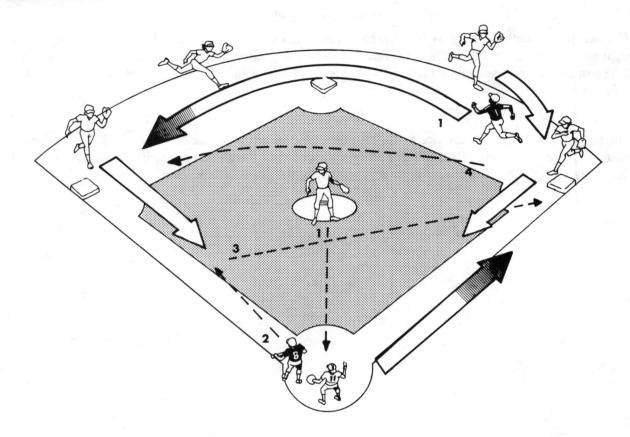

The purpose of this play is to place a sacrifice bunt on the ground in such a way that the first-base runner can be advanced all the way to third base. This is a shocking play. The defense never expects a runner to try for two bases on a bunt; the play depends on their neglect of third base. Success for this bunt play should be 50 percent if the first-base runner is very fast.

Play Progression and Analysis

- First-base runner knows he is going from first to third on the bunt. Special sign is given.
- Batter gets the "sacrifice-two bases along" sign. Batter must bunt the ball 30 feet in line with third base. A slow, soft bunt is required.
- Batter hopes for a pitch slightly inside.
- Runner on first base is also given the steal-on-pitcher sign from the coach. This is a stealing play, too.
- Runner must have a big lead and a big jump to make it from first to third base.
- Bunt dies in the grass. Third baseman comes in to field the ball. As the throw is made for the out at first base, the runner rounds second base. Third base is not guarded by anyone. First-base runner sees this and does not slow down.
- He makes it into third base easily. Even if third base is guarded, the throw from first will arrive too late.

Timing Analysis

(Assuming third base was guarded)

Time of ball from contact on bat to fielding by third baseman = 2.80 seconds
Third baseman's throw to first base   = 1.40 seconds

First baseman's hesitation	= 0.80 seconds
First baseman's throw to third base	= 1.80 seconds
The total time of all of the above	= 6.80 seconds
Time of first-base runner's run from first to third base	= 6.60 seconds

If the defense makes no miscues, then the first-base runner arrives at third base 0.2 seconds ahead of the ball (assuming some infielder remembers to cover third base). In high school ball, a team usually forgets to cover.

Defensing the Play

This play depends upon the defense forgetting to cover third base on a sacrifice situation. In practice, be sure the pitcher always covers third base whenever third baseman plays a bunt. Whoever does not play a bunt on the left side of the infield should always run to cover third base.

Helpful Tips

This play depends upon the first-base runner getting a big lead and a big jump on the pitcher. Also, the runner knows that if the bunt is not to third baseman, or if the ball is bobbled, he should stay on second base.

Play 22: Safe-Squeeze Bunt

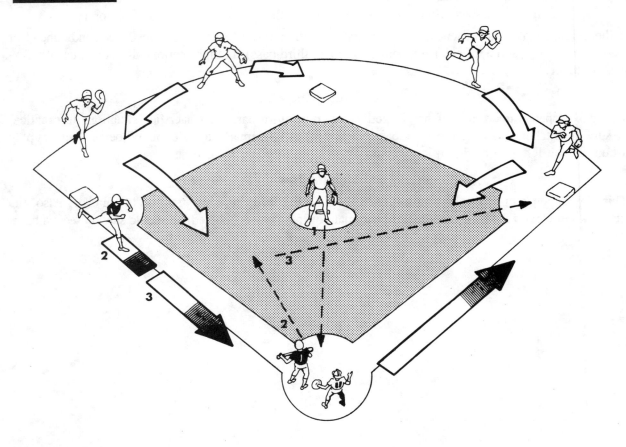

The purpose of this type of bunt is to score a run from third base by bunting without making an out. The runner will come home, but only if it is a good bunt the runner thinks he can beat. This play does not have much element of surprise. All teams know it and expect it. Many teams use it as a part of their bunting repertoires. The success rate should be 60 percent, if the third-base runner is fast and the batter is a good bunter.

Play Progression and Analysis

- Batter gets safe-squeeze sign from the coach. Third-base runner sees the same sign.
- Do not give the third-base runner any kind of suicide-squeeze or steal sign. It isn't a suicide or a real steal.
- Third-base runner goes home fast only if ball is slowly bunted between the pitcher and first base or between the pitcher and third base.
- If ball is bunted badly, third-base runner should come very far off third and bluff a break home. If infielder throws to first base to get the bunter out, third-base runner has the option to either try to make it to the plate or go back to third.

Timing Analysis

(If bunt is good and throw is made to first base)

Time of throw from third baseman to first base = 1.40 seconds
Time of hesitation by the first baseman = 0.70 seconds
Time of throw from first baseman to home = 1.40 seconds
Total of all of the above = 3.50 seconds

Time of third-base runner's run to home   = 3.20 seconds

If the defense makes no miscues, then the third-base runner (who is 20 feet off the base) will arrive at home plate 0.3 seconds ahead of the ball.

Defensing the Play

If the infielder sees the third-base runner holding, he should fire to first base and yell, "Watch home," or the infielder can fake a throw to first, then pick off the runner at third base.

Helpful Tips

Third-base runner must take a big lead while determining if the bunt is good. If it is an excellent bunt, the runner breaks for home immediately, or the runner can hold his position and break as the throw is made to first base.

Play 23: Suicide-Squeeze Bunt to Score One Run

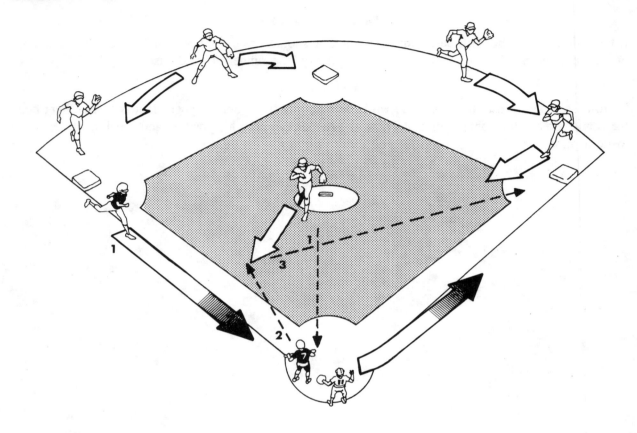

The purpose of this play is to score only the third-base runner. He breaks for home on the pitch, and the batter must lay down a fair bunt. The defense feels helpless as the bunt is laid down fair, for there is no defense against the unexpected suicide squeeze. If the bunt is good, the run scores. This is simply a steal home with help from the bunter. Success rate on suicide-squeeze bunts is 75 percent.

Play Progression and Analysis

- Tell the third-base runner not to commit himself down third-base line until the pitcher has committed himself to the batter. Keep the pitcher guessing.
- Batter and runner must both see and understand both signs given to them by the coach.
- Batter gets suicide sign from coach.
- Runner gets steal-on-pitcher sign from the coach.
- Batter must just bunt it softly anywhere in fair territory.
- Batter should square around to bunt just as pitcher is coming down in his delivery.
- If bunt is missed, third-base runner must take out the catcher.
- If pitcher is in stretch, avoid a third-base pickoff and have runner shorten his lead before breaking for the plate.

Timing Analysis

None applies here. On a suicide squeeze, the third-base runner is not in a race with the ball to get to a base. But if the bunter misses the ball, the third-base runner will surely be tagged out.

Defensing the Play

The standard procedure is to throw the ball right at the batter. As the batter gets out of the way, the catcher has the ball, and the tag is made on the runner. Another defense is to call for a pitchout, but a ball too far outside may be hard to bring back to the plate for a good tag if the runner is fast and gets an early break. The best defense against a squeeze bunt is to throw very fast pitches, curves, sliders, or any ball difficult to bunt. Perhaps the bunter will hit a pop-up and give the defense a double play.

Helpful Tips

This is a higher-risk play. The batter must bunt or even throw the bat out at a bad pitch to at least foul it off. Runner must slide hard. Tell the batter to just get the ball down anywhere on the ground. There is no need here to be fancy and place the bunt in a particular spot—just get it down fair.

Play 24: Suicide-Squeeze Bunt to Score Two Runs

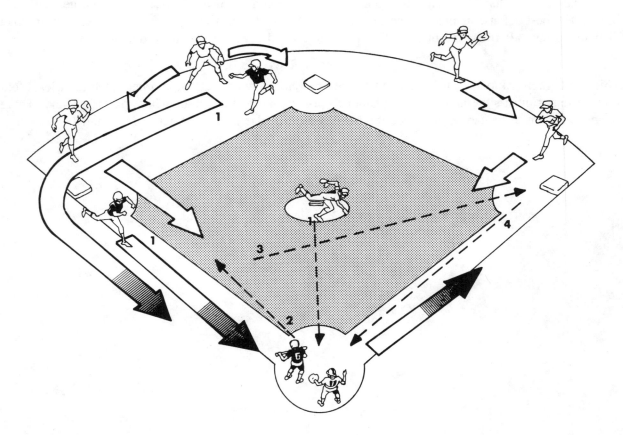

The purpose of this play is to score the runners on second and third bases. Both runners break for the next base on the pitch, and the batter must lay down a fair bunt. This is baseball's premier running play. It shocks the minds of the opponents. Scoring two runs on one bunt is almost unheard of in the game, but it is not that difficult to do. The success rate for this double suicide play is 60 percent, high enough to warrant trying the play more often than it is normally attempted.

Play Progression and Analysis

- It is important that the second- and third-base runners do not commit themselves to steals until the pitcher brings his arm down to deliver.
- Both batter and runner must see and understand both signs given by the coach.
- Batter gets a special "suicide-squeeze, score two runners" sign from coach.
- Both runners get steal-on-pitcher sign and see the sign to the batter.
- Batter must try to place a very soft, dead bunt in a particular spot, on a line to third base and 30 feet from the plate.
- Batter should square around to bunt just as pitcher is coming down in the delivery.
- If the bunt is missed, third-base runner must take out the catcher and second-base runner must stop at third base.
- If bunt is good, but bobbled or not hit to third baseman, the second-base runner stops at third base.

Timing Analysis

(Assuming third baseman fields the bunt and second-base runner tries for home)

Time of pitch to batter	= 0.90 seconds
Time of ball from bat to third baseman's pickup	= 2.80 seconds
Time of third baseman's throw to first base	= 1.30 seconds
Time of hesitation of first baseman	= 0.90 seconds
Time of throw from first baseman to home	= 1.40 seconds
Total time of all of the above	= 7.30 seconds
Time of second-base runner to home	= 6.70 seconds

If the defense makes no miscues, the second-base runner will arrive at the plate 0.6 seconds ahead of the ball.

Defensing the Play

Standard procedure is to throw the ball right at the batter. As batter gets out of the way, catcher gets the pitch and tags runner out easily. Another defense is to call for a pitchout, but a ball pitched too far outside may be hard to bring back to the plate for a good tag. To prevent both runs from scoring on a squeeze, be certain pitcher holds the second-base runner closer to second base before you pitch. This will cut down his early break for home plate. The best defense against a squeeze bunt is to throw very fast pitches, curves, sliders, or any ball difficult to bunt. Perhaps the bunter will pop up the ball and thus hit into a double *or even a triple play*.

Helpful Tips

Done correctly, this play does the same damage as a home run with one man on base—but the ball never leaves the infield. The batter must just touch the ball with bat, and the runner on second base must have a great lead. Tell the bunter to put the ball down in fair territory. This assures at least one run of scoring. If the batter is an excellent bunter and can lay a soft one in line with third base, then both runs should score.

Play 25: Fake Bunt and Slash With a Man on First or Second Base

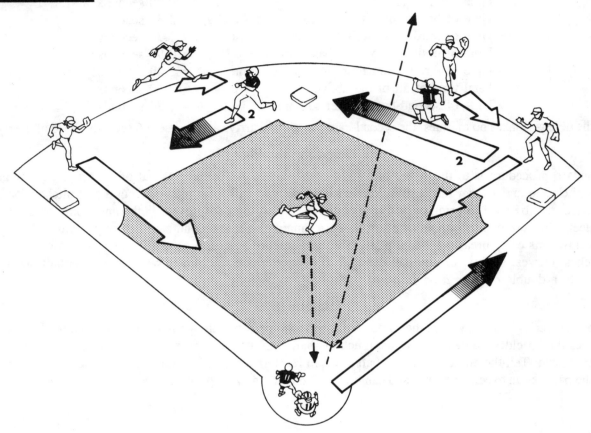

The purpose of this play is to swing at a pitch with a slash motion, a reluctant half-swing. It looks like a bunt or fake-bunt play at first; then the bat is drawn back as the ball is pitched. Finally, the bat punches at the ball, attempting to get good contact. Advantages of this play are several. The infield is drawn in by the batter's fake-bunt stance, but the fielders then find the ball popped over them for a lazy base hit. This can move an alert base runner two bases along if the ball is well placed. Since bat control is especially difficult to teach younger players, a success rate of only 25 percent can be expected.

Play Progression and Analysis

- Batter gets the sign from the coach for the fake bunt and slash.
- Batter squares around to bunt very early, with his bat out level to the ground. He grips the bat in such a way that his hands are also ready to use the bat to hit.
- Just as the pitcher's arm comes down in his delivery, the batter draws bat back to a hitting position, but keeps it in front of his body. He is going to punch the ball.
- Runners on base watch the hit ball, but they do not steal on the pitch.
- However, if the ball clears the infield on the fly or is a slow roller, runners slide into the next base, or possibly advance two bases.

Timing Analysis

None.

Defensing the Play

This is one of baseball's hardest plays to defense. The defense does not know until the last moment what the batter will do. The defense must shift to cover a possible bunt, but after the batter moves back into a semihitting stance, the defense hasn't time to shift back to the proper defensive position.

Helpful Tips

This play is obviously designed to get the defense to creep in and move around, creating holes to hit through. The hitter then punches a ball over or through the infield, moving the runners one or two bases. Practice daily with each batter to look at holes created by shifting infielders. Hard work will teach players to pop a soft hit over or through the holes. Players will take pride in learning bat control.

Play 26: Fake Bunt and Slash With a Man on Third Base

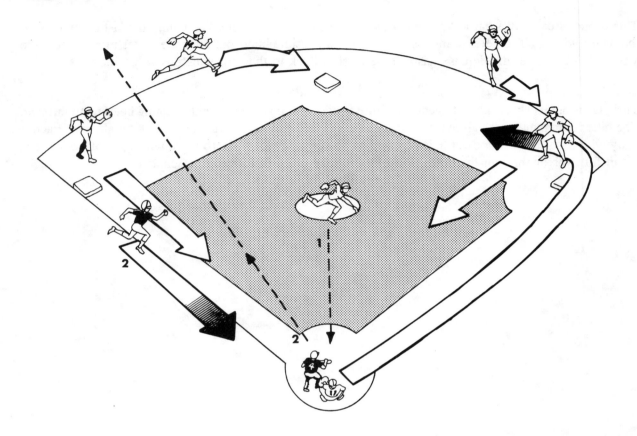

The purpose and technique of this play are identical to Play 25, except that this one scores a run. Because bat control is difficult for younger players, a success rate of only 25 percent can be expected.

Play Progression and Analysis

- Batter gets the sign for the fake bunt and slash. Runner gets the same sign. This is not a steal play.
- Batter squares around to bunt very early, holding the bat out level to the ground. He must grip the bat, however, so his hands are also ready to use the bat to hit.
- Just as the pitcher's arm comes down in his delivery, batter draws bat to a hitting position, but keeps it in front of his body. He is going to punch the ball.
- Runner on third base watches the hit ball. If it clears the infield on the fly or is a slow roller, he comes home.
- Batter does not have to swing at a bad pitch.

Timing Analysis

None.

Defensing the Play

The defense does not know until the last moment what the batter will do. The defense must shift to cover a possible bunt, but after the batter moves back into a semihitting stance, the defense hasn't time to shift back to proper defensive position.

Helpful Tips

Practice daily with each batter to look at holes created by shifting infielders. Hard work will teach players to pop a soft hit over or through the holes.

Play 27: Fake Bunt With a Man on Second Base

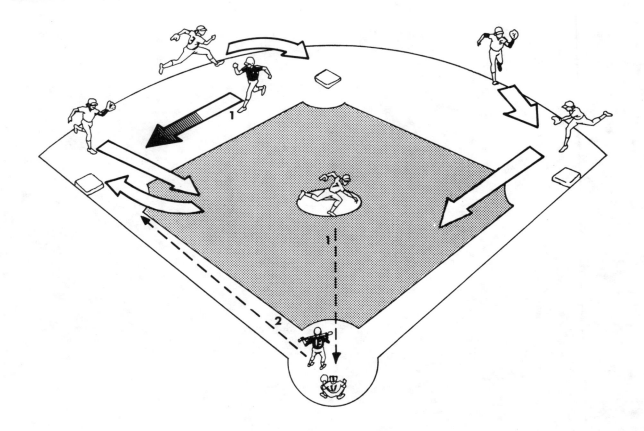

This play is a clever way to assist the second-base runner to steal third base. The batter assists his team-mate in this effort. The play is designed to fool the third baseman who likes to creep in too far to get an edge on the bunting play he believes is coming up. He moves in too far and cannot get back to cover his base when the catcher tries to throw out the stealing runner. This play is definitely a steal play. The second-base runner must have a good lead.

Successful execution not only results in a stolen base, but often causes the errant catcher's throw to sail into left field, allowing a run to score. Success rate on this play is 50 percent.

Play Progression and Analysis

- Batter gets sign for fake bunt.
- Runner gets the steal-on-pitcher sign.
- Both the runner and the batter must see both signs.
- Batter squares around to bunt very, very early. Batter puts the bat out and levels it to the ground.
- Batter watches the ball sail past the bat, but doesn't let it touch the bat.
- Batter brings the bat in from the bunting position, but rather slowly. He doesn't want to physically interfere with catcher. The bat will create a visual hazard for the catcher, and it may slow down his throw to the base.
- Runner takes off with the pitch, slides hard into the next base, and gets up fast.

Timing Analysis

Time of pitch to batter	= 0.90 seconds
Time of catcher hesitation	= 0.50 seconds
Time of catcher throw to third base	= 1.30 seconds
Total of all of the above	= 2.70 seconds
Time of runner's run from second to third base	= 3.20 seconds

If the defense makes no miscues, then the ball should arrive at third base about 0.5 seconds ahead of the runner. However, there will be no one covering third base to take the throw, even if the runner is late.

Defensing the Play

It is very hard to defense. Until the last moment, the defense must be ready for a bunt. Defensive men are all shifting to cover bases on a bunt. The best defense is a good catcher's arm. Third baseman is all alone here to cover the base. Third baseman must be taught to be able to sprint back to base to cover and not creep in too far. Even then, it will be a difficult moving target at which the catcher throws. The third baseman will have trouble taking the throw and making a good tag.

Helpful Tips

This play attempts to get the third baseman to creep in too far. Be sure to alert the second-base runner to slide into third base, get up quickly, and be ready to go home on an overthrow or a muffed play by the third baseman.

Play 28: Fake Bunt With a Man on First Base

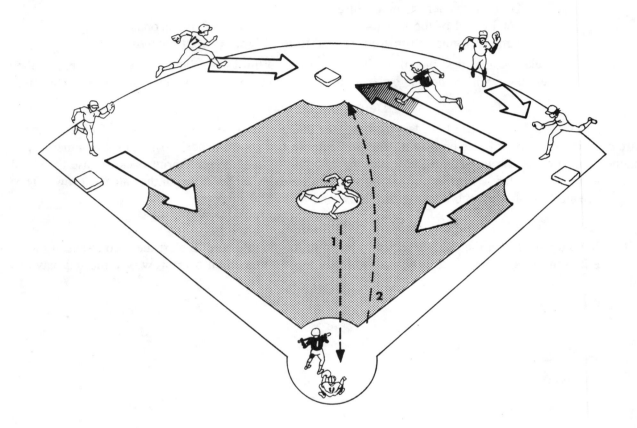

This play is a clever way to assist the first-base runner to steal second base. The batter assists his team-mate in this effort. The opponent must guess whether the team will bunt or fake bunt. This play is designed simply to get the bat in the eyes of the catcher in order to slow his throw or cause it to be off target. This tactic is definitely a steal play. The first-base runner is going on the pitch. He must have a good lead. The running team will advance a runner without sacrificing an out. Success rate is high at 60 percent.

Play Progression and Analysis

- Batter gets the sign for fake bunt, and the runner gets the steal-on-pitcher sign.
- Both runner and batter must see each other's signs.
- Batter squares around to bunt very early. He puts his bat out and levels it to the ground.
- Batter watches ball sail past the bat, but he doesn't let it touch the bat.
- Batter brings the bat in from his bunting position, but rather slowly. He doesn't want to physically interfere with the catcher. The bat will give a visual hazard to the catcher and may slow his throw to second base.
- Runner takes off with the pitch, slides hard into the next base, and gets up fast.

Timing Analysis

Time of pitch to batter	= 0.90 seconds
Time of catcher hesitation	= 0.50 seconds
Time of catcher throw to second base	= 1.75 seconds

| Total of all of the above | = 3.15 seconds |
| Time of runner's run from first to second base | = 3.20 seconds |

If the defense makes no miscues, then the ball should arrive at second base 0.05 seconds ahead of the runner. However, to throw out the runner, catcher must have a quick release and be on target.

Defensing the Play

Until the last moment, the defense must be ready for a bunt. Defensive players must shift to cover bases on a bunt. The best defense is a good catcher's arm. But this play is always hard to stop.

Chapter

3

The Official Rules of Running

Every ball player can become a good base runner— but only if he knows the rules. Yet many coaches spend too little time in this area, assuming players already know enough about the rules of the running game or that time spent on instruction won't pay off. Both assumptions are usually false. Often the only man on the diamond who knows these rules as every player should know them is the umpire.

To assist the coach and player in correcting this deficiency, this chapter cites verbatim every sub-rule from Section 7.0, entitled "Running," from the 1987 *Official Baseball Rules* compiled by the National Rules Committee of the American and National Leagues and the National High School Federation (the original page number from the *Rules* book follows each rule, in parentheses). A condensed, simplified interpretation follows each rule. Next, a "Hints and Tips" section gives special directions and warnings regarding pitfalls. Finally, a drills section presents original techniques developed by Jim McGarry, former baseball coach at San Bernardino Valley College, and by the author for teaching players the official rules.

Section 7.0: The Runner

Rule as Stated: 7.01

A runner acquires the right to an unoccupied base when the runner touches it before the runner is out. The runner is then entitled to it until the runner is put out or forced to vacate it for another runner legally entitled to that base. (p. 29)

Condensed Rule: The runner first earns the right to any base. He may keep it unless touched with the ball when off the base or forced to move on.

Hints and Tips: Runners are always forced to move when

- they are on first,
- runners are on first and second, or
- the bases are loaded.

Coach's Rules Drill: Be certain the coach explains the rule number and the reason for each drill. Give the correct umpire's decision after the play is over. Coach hits balls to all parts of diamond. Runners run bases according to the hit and the rules of good running. Coach acts as umpire on each play.

Rule as Stated: 7.02

In advancing, a runner shall touch first, second, third, and home base in that order. If forced to return, runner shall retouch all bases in reverse order. If the ball is dead under any provision or rule, Section 5.09, then the runner may go directly to his base. (p. 29)

Condensed Rule: Bases must be touched in order. Bases must be retouched in reverse order. If runners have advanced several bases on a dead ball, they may go directly back to the first or original base.

Hints and Tips: Instruct runners to actually touch each bag in the necessary order.

Coach's Rules Drill: (a) Coach hits singles, doubles, triples. Runners touch all bases. On the next round use the same drill, but as the runner reaches his farthest base, he reverses and touches every base back to first. (b) With a runner on first the coach hits a deep fly. Forgetting the correct number of outs, the runner steals on the pitch. He goes all the way to third base and then reverses and comes back to first base, attempting to beat the relay throw. The coach makes the calls.

Rule as Stated: 7.03

Two runners may not occupy the same base. But if, while the ball is alive, two runners are touching a base, the following runner shall be out when tagged. The runner entitled to the base is the preceding runner. (p. 29)

Condensed Rule: Remember, it is the *following* runner who is out when tagged. First, runners must avoid occupying the same base. This can be avoided easily by reminding all runners to run with head and eyes up, aware of what is happening ahead.

Hints and Tips: Be sure, in this situation, that the preceding runner does not move off the base and cause a double-play tag.

Coach's Rules Drill: Put men on any two bases you wish. The following runner should run to the base where the lead runner is. Both runners must stay on the base. The nearest baseman gets the throw from the catcher. Baseman goes over and tags both runners. The coach makes the call, indicating who stays and who is out. The lead runner does not move from the base. Either the catcher or pitcher can initiate the play, throwing to the baseman nearest the two runners.

Rule as Stated: 7.04 (a)

Each runner, other than the batter, may, without the liability to be put out, advance one base when there is a balk called. (p. 29)

Condensed Rule: When umpire raises hand and calls balk, any runner on any base advances. This rule does not affect the batter.

Hints and Tips: Instruct runners, when they think balk has been called, to wait for the umpire to motion them toward the next base.

Coach's Rules Drill: Have team members on the bases in various combinations. Take normal leads. Have the pitcher balk in different ways (as found in rules Section 8.05). Have the runners advance one base as the coach makes the umpire's call. Teach runners on this drill the most common balks opposing pitchers will make.

Rule as Stated: 7.04 (b)

Each runner, except batter, may advance one base when the batter's advance without liability to be put out forces the runner to vacate his base or when the batter hits a fair ball that touches another runner or the umpire before such ball has been touched by, or has passed a fielder, if the runner is forced to advance. (p. 29)

Condensed Rule: Runners are forced to advance only one base. If the following runner or batter is entitled to a base, then they are entitled to advance only one base.

Hints and Tips: Force plays entitle runners to only one base at a time. Runners go beyond one base at their own peril.

Coach's Rules Drill: (a) Put man on first. Hit grounders where only a force at second is possible. Runners should slide. Batter is safe at first. Instruct the hitter how to run first base on this play. (b) Have a player act as umpire. He should stand between two bases in the umpire's usual position. Hit slow bouncer at umpire and let it hit him. Call the play and advance the runner.

Rule as Stated: 7.04 (c)

Each runner, except the batter, may advance one base when a fielder, after catching the ball on the fly, falls into a bench or a stand, or falls across ropes into a crowd when spectators are on the field. If a fly is caught in the dugout by a fielder, ball is in play after the catch. If fielder falls into stands or dugout, all runners advance one base. (p. 29)

Condensed Rule: On a caught fly, runners are awarded next base only if the fielder falls into the stands or benches.

Hints and Tips: If the fly is caught in the dugout, runners advance after catch at their own peril. Runners are not awarded next base.

Coach's Rules Drill: Place runners in different positions on bases. Throw high flies near the stands. Infielders should catch the fly and fake falling into stands. Make the call and advance each runner one base.

Rule as Stated: 7.04 (d)

Each batter, except the runner, may advance one base, when runner is attempting to steal a base, and the batter is interfered with by the catcher or any other fielder. (p. 29)

Condensed Rule: If the catcher steps up over the plate, touches the bat with his glove or equipment, or pushes batter out of the way during a pitch, interference is called. Batter is awarded first base. This usually occurs as the catcher moves up in the box during a bunt or fake-bunt attempt.

Hints and Tips: Equal responsibility rests with the batter. He may not interfere with the catcher's play on the runner after the batter has swung, attempted a bunt, or taken the pitch.

Coach's Rules Drill: Put runners on various bases. After a pitch, the catcher should interfere with the batter in various ways as the runner steals. Catcher should then throw down to the next base. Call the play and award the runners the bases. Each runner moves up one base, including the third-base runner, who scores.

Rule as Stated: 7.05 (a)

Each runner, including the batter-runner, may, without liability to be put out, advance to home base, scoring a run, if a fair ball goes out of the playing field in flight and runners touch all bases in order, or, if a fair ball, in the umpire's judgment, would have gone out of the playing field in flight, is deflected by the act of a fielder in throwing his glove, cap, or any article of apparel. (p. 29)

Condensed Rule: This is the standard home-run rule. Runners slowly touch each base in order without threat of being tagged out.

Hints and Tips: Batter should run as hard as possible in case the ball hits the fence, is caught and dropped, or is not judged a home run by the umpire.

Coach's Rules Drill: Hit home runs over the fence. Batter rounds bases slowly and touches each one. Make sure runner touches each base. Next, hit home runs over the fence. Have the batter miss the base designated by the coach. After the runner sits down, the defense should work an appeal play at the base not touched. Appeal to the umpire, the coach in this case.

Rule as Stated: 7.05 (b)

Each runner, including the batter-runner, may, without liability to be put out, advance three bases if a fielder will deliberately touch any fair ball with a cap, mask, or any other part of the uniform detached from its proper place on the person. The ball is in play, and the batter may advance to home base at his peril. (p. 30)

Condensed Rule: Whether ball is a fly or grounder, all runners, including the batter, go three bases if a fielder plays the ball improperly with his equipment.

Hints and Tips: Before going to third, the batter must verify that the umpire indicates the number of bases to be awarded. Be sure it is not a two-base award.

Coach's Rules Drill: Put men on various bases and hit balls all over the diamond. A defensive man should field the ball by reaching up and hitting it with his cap. The catcher can touch a slow roller with the mask on several tries. Call the play. Each runner will advance three bases, including the batter.

Rule as Stated: 7.05 (c)

Each runner, including the batter-runner, may, without liability to be put out, advance three bases, if a fielder will deliberately throw a glove at and touch a fair ball. The ball is in play, and the batter may advance to home base at his own peril. (p. 30)

Condensed Rule: If a fielder throws his glove and touches a fair ball, the runners are given a three-base award. This does not apply if the glove misses the hit ball.

Hints and Tips: The batter, before going to third, must verify the number of bases awarded. Be sure it is not a two-base award.

Coach's Rules Drill: Put runners on various bases. Hit balls all over the diamond. Have the player who fields the ball throw his glove at the ball and hit it. Call the play. Each runner advances three bases, including the batter.

Rule as Stated: 7.05 (d)

Each runner, including the batter-runner, may, without liability to be put out, advance two bases, if a fielder will deliberately touch a thrown ball with the cap, mask, or any other part of the uniform detached from its proper place on the player. The ball is in play. (p. 30)

Condensed Rule: This must be a thrown ball, not a hit ball. If a thrown ball hits fielders' equipment that is not where it should be, two bases are awarded to each runner.

Hints and Tips: Batter should stop at second base, after the umpire has waved him to that base. Do not move off first base until indicated by the umpire.

Coach's Rules Drill: Put runners on various bases. Direct certain players to throw to certain bases after fielding a grounder. Each thrower is to throw wide to the base. Have the baseman take off his cap and try to stop the ball with it. Call the play. Each runner advances two bases, including the batter.

Rule as Stated: 7.05 (e)

Each runner, including the batter-runner, may, without the liability to be put out, advance two bases, if a fielder deliberately throws the glove at and touches a thrown ball. The ball is in play. However, there is no penalty if the ball is not touched. This rule does not apply if the glove is carried off the hand by the force of a batted or thrown ball, or when the glove slips off the hand while player is trying to make an obvious effort on a legitimate catch. (p. 30)

Condensed Rule: This must be a thrown ball, not a hit ball. If a fielder throws his glove and touches a thrown ball, then all runners, including the batter, move forward two bases.

Hints and Tips: Have the batter pull up at second base after the umpire has waved him to that base. Do not move off first base until the umpire does this.

Coach's Rules Drill: Same as previous drill except the baseman covering a base on a wide throw will throw the glove at the ball thrown. Be sure the ball is hit by the glove. Call the play. Each runner advances two bases, including the batter.

Rule as Stated: 7.05 (f)

Each runner, including the batter-runner, may, without the liability to be put out, advance two bases, if a fair ball bounces or is deflected into the stands outside the first or third base foul line, or, if it goes through or under a field fence, or through or under shrubbery or vines on the fence, scoreboard, shrubbery, or vines. (p. 30)

Condensed Rule: If a fair ball passes first or third base, then bounces hard and into the stands or under an outfield or foul area fence, each runner may advance two bases.

Hints and Tips: In these cases, where ball cannot be retrieved, keep running to home plate. Umpire will wave runner back to second base if necessary.

Coach's Rules Drill: Place runners on various bases. Coach should hit hard balls down the line or in the power alley where there is room under a fence. Make the call. All runners should keep going home. The batter advances only as far as second base. Umpire will direct the other runners back to the correct bases.

Rule as Stated: 7.05 (g)

Each runner, including the batter-runner, may, without the liability to be put out, advance two bases, when, with no spectators on the playing field, a thrown ball goes into the stands, or into a bench, whether or not it rebounds back onto the field, or over, or under, or through a field fence, or on the slanting part of the screen above the backstop, or remains in the meshes of a wire screen protecting the spectators. The ball is dead. When such a wild throw is the first play by the infielder, the umpire, in awarding such bases, shall be governed by the position of the runners at the time the ball was pitched. At all other times, the umpire shall be governed by the position of the runners at the time the wild throw was made. (p. 30)

Condensed Rule: This is the famous "One-and-One Rule." Runners get the base to which they were going, plus one more. Usually, this occurs on a throw made after fielding a hit ball.

Hints and Tips: The safe thing on this play is for each runner to advance one base only, then wait for the umpire to award the next base.

Coach's Rules Drill: First, put runners on first and second bases. Hit the ball to any infielder. Fielder should throw over the first baseman into the stands. Award each runner one base, plus the base he was approaching. Second, place runners on any bases. Give the ball to each infielder and have him throw over the head of first or third baseman. Runners should move up one base and wait for umpire to award another base.

Rule as Stated: 7.05 (h)

Each runner, including the batter-runner, may, without the liability to be put out, advance one base, if a ball, pitched to the batter, or thrown by the pitcher from the position on the pitcher's plate to a base to catch a runner, goes into a stand or bench, or over or through a field fence or backstop. (p. 31)

Condensed Rule: This play starts and ends with the pitcher. It applies only to a pitcher's thrown ball, while he is on the mound.

Hints and Tips: Just advance one base and stay.

Coach's Rules Drill: Give ball to pitcher. While in the stretch, or completely off the mound, the pitcher suddenly throws over first and third into the stands. Award each runner one base. (Runners wait for the award of the base from the umpire.)

Rule as Stated: 7.05 (i)

Each runner, including the batter-runner, may, without the liability to be put out, advance one base, if the batter becomes a runner on ball four or strike three, when the pitch passes the catcher and lodges in the umpire's mask or paraphernalia. If batter has strike three or ball four, and he goes to first on wild pitch, he is entitled to first base only. (p. 31)

Condensed Rule: Applies only to umpire's equipment. This rule is intended to cover the unusual occurrence of the ball lodging in the umpire's equipment. All runners, including the batter, move up one base.

Hints and Tips: Runners and batter wait to be awarded their bases.

Coach's Rules Drill: This is not a practical situation for a drill. Percentage of incidence is very low.

Rule as Stated: 7.06 (a)

"Obstruction Called"—when obstruction occurs, the umpire shall call or signal "Obstruction." If a play is being made on the obstructed runner, or if the batter-runner is obstructed before runner touches first base, the ball is dead and all runners shall advance, without liability to be put out, to the bases that would have been reached, in the umpire's judgment, if there had been no obstruction. The obstructed runner shall be awarded at least one base beyond the base he had last legally touched before the obstruction. Any preceding runners, forced to advance by the award of bases as the penalty for obstruction, shall advance without liability to be put out. (p. 31)

Condensed Rule: Each runner is awarded one base. The batter receives a base only if he is on the way to first. A runner who is obstructed by defense shall advance to his next base. If this advancement forces other runners, they each advance one base.

Hints and Tips: Runners play it safe and wait for the umpire to wave them to the next base.

Coach's Rules Drill: Have men on various bases. Hit slow grounders to the infielders. Designate the pitcher or catcher to get in path of advancing runner. Call obstruction. Each runner advances one base beyond the last one. Batter is awarded first base on the obstruction.

Rule as Stated: 7.06 (b)

When obstruction occurs, the umpire shall call or signal "Obstruction." If no play is being made on the obstructed runner, the play shall proceed until no further action is possible. The umpire shall then call time and impose such penalties, if any, as in his judgment will nullify the act of obstruction. (p. 31)

Condensed Rule: Umpire waits until the play is over to call obstruction, then decides the penalties.

Hints and Tips: Runners should wait on the bag reached at the end of the play until umpire assesses the penalties and awards the correct bases.

Coach's Rules Drill: Have men on various bases. Hit slow grounders to infielders. Designate different infielders to get in the path of designated runners. Call time after the play is over. The runners move up one base each.

Rule as Stated: 7.07

If, with a runner on third base, and trying to score by means of a squeeze play or a steal, the catcher or any other fielder steps on or in front of home base without possession of the ball, or touches the batter or his bat, the pitcher shall be charged with a balk and the batter shall be awarded first base on the interference, and the ball is dead. (p. 32)

Condensed Rule: The runner on third base scores on the balk. The batter is awarded first base and the third-base runner advances one base. Any other runners will advance one base by the balk rule.

Hints and Tips: The umpire will award batter first base. Wait for the base to be awarded.

Coach's Rules Drill: Have men on third base alternate between an attempt to steal home and a squeeze play on each pitch. Have catcher either step on plate, touch or shove the batter, or deflect the bat. Call interference. All runners should move up one base. The third-base runner scores, and the batter is awarded first base.

Rule as Stated: 7.08 (a)

Any runner is out when running more than three feet away from a direct line between the bases to avoid being tagged, unless the action is to avoid interference with a fielder fielding a batted ball, or, after reaching first base, runner leaves the baseline, obviously abandoning an effort to touch the next base. (p. 32)

Condensed Rule: The only exception is avoiding interference with a man fielding a ball. This rule defines the baseline limits and specifies when the base runner may leave these limits in moving from base to base.

Hints and Tips: Wide turns at all bases are allowed.

Coach's Rules Drill: With runners at the plate, hit the ball to all infielders. First, have the runner run outside baseline, not between lanes. Second, station the first baseman as if he were taking a pop-up. Direct runner to run around baseman, then to first base. Finally, have the runner run the line and go sit down. The call is safe. If the first baseman touches the base, the call is out.

Rule as Stated: 7.08 (b)

Any runner is out when intentionally interfering with a thrown ball or hindering a fielder attempting to make a play on a batted ball. (p. 32)

Condensed Rule: This rule refers to both thrown and batted balls. The rule means that no runner must impede the normal thrown ball or the fielding of a batted ball by a fielder. Runner's best rule is to stay out of the line of all balls thrown or hit.

Hints and Tips: Runners should not permit a situation where umpire has to decide.

Coach's Rules Drill: First, have runners get caught in a rundown between first and second. Have baseman make a soft throw, not a lob. Runner should duck into the path of ball. Call the runner out. Next, put a runner on second base. Place the shortstop in normal fielding position. Hit good bouncer to shortstop. Runner intentionally gets in front of shortstop and permits ball to hit him. Call him out.

Rule as Stated: 7.08 (c)

Any runner is out when tagged, while the ball is live, off a base. Exception: The one exception to this rule is that a batter-runner who has over-run or overslid first base on a run from home plate cannot be tagged out if returning to the base immediately. Also, if the impact of a runner breaks a base loose from its position, no play can be made on that runner, as that base has been reached safely. (p. 32)

Condensed Rule: Runner must return to first base down the line immediately, if he has run across first base on a close play. The rule warns all runners that any tag with the ball while runner is off base is an out.

Hints and Tips: Umpire will call time and fix the bag if it is loosened and moves.

Coach's Rules Drill: Place runner on second base and have him steal third on the pitch. The catcher should throw slowly to third base. Runner slides into the bag, which has been left unanchored. Runner should then scramble back to where bag should be and touch it. Call runner safe.

Rule as Stated: 7.08 (d)

Any runner is out when failing to retouch a base after a fair ball or foul ball is legally caught, before runner, or his base, is tagged by a fielder. Runner shall not be called out for failure to retouch a base after the first following pitch has been made, or the first following play or attempted play has been made. This is an appeal play. (p. 33)

Condensed Rule: If ball reaches the runner's original base before runner does, he is out. The runner must know that on all flies, fair or foul, he is obligated to return to the last base and touch it before the ball is relayed back to that base.

Hints and Tips: This occurs if the runner forgets the number of outs and advances too far.

Coach's Rules Drill: (a) With a runner on second base, hit deep flies to the outfield. Direct the runner to leave too early, and land on third base. Defense should appeal and run an appeal play. Call the runner out at second base. (b) With a runner on third base, practice the drill as above, but have the runner come in to score. Pitcher should pitch one ball. The defense then appeals the play. Runner is called safe, and the appeal is denied.

Rule as Stated: 7.08 (e)

Any runner is out when failing to reach the next base before a fielder tags runner or the base, after runner has been forced to advance by reason of the batter becoming a runner. But if a following runner is put out on a force play, the force is removed and the advance runner must be tagged to be put out. This, in baseball, will result in what is called the "Reverse Double Play." If a runner is running into a base to which runner is forced, then overslides it or overruns it, the runner must be tagged to be put out. However, if the forced runner, after touching the base that he was forced to, retreats for any reason towards the last base, then the force play is reinstated and can again be put out if the defense tags the base to which runner is forced. (p. 33)

Condensed Rule: Runner never knows when he may be the front end of a "Reverse Double Play;" therefore, always slide when forced on a ground ball. If runner overslides a base, he must reach back and touch it before baseman, with the ball, touches the base.

Hints and Tips: First-base runner should always go hard on a ground ball and break up the attempted double play.

Coach's Rules Drill: (a) With runners on second and third base, the coach hits hard grounders to the infield. The defense forces man at third or second. Runners should stay on the bases to which they were forced until called out or safe. (b) Another drill begins with runners on second and first. Hit hard grounder to first baseman near his bag. First baseman touches first, then fires the throw to second. All infielders yell "Tag!" Runner slides into second base and waits on the base for coach to make the call.

Rule as Stated: 7.08 (f)

Any runner is out when touched by a fair hit ball in fair territory before the ball has touched or passed an infielder. The ball is dead, and no runner may score, nor may runners advance, except runners forced to advance. If a runner is touched by an infield fly coming down, runner is not out, but the batter is automatically out. If two runners should be touched by the same fair hit ball on the same play, only the first man hit is called out, and the ball is dead. However, if a runner is off his base and touched by an infield fly coming down, then both batter and the runner are out. Double play on one fly. (p. 33)

Condensed Rule: Runners do not let a fair fly or grounder touch them at any time. This rule explains that only the first runner touched by a hit ball shall be called out. The ball is always dead on a play where a hit ball touches the runner.

Hints and Tips: If ball has touched or passed an infielder, the hit runner may advance any number of bases.

Coach's Rules Drill: With runners at all bases, hit slow bouncers right at the runners. When a runner is hit, yell "Time" and "You're out!" The ball is dead. The hit runner is out and all other runners should go back to bases previously occupied.

Rule as Stated: 7.08 (g)

Any runner is out when attempting to score on a play in which the batter interferes with the play at home base before two are out. The runner is out, not the batter. The batter stays up there if less than two outs. If there are two outs in the preceding case, then the batter is out and no score counts and the inning is over. (p. 33)

Condensed Rule: Batters must quickly get out of the way of runners trying to score. Remember that the third-base runner is out, not the batter. The team loses the run on this attempt.

Hints and Tips: The penalty is great for such interference. The batting team loses the out and the run.

Coach's Rules Drill: Place a runner on third base. Pitcher pitches and batter interferes in various ways with catcher as the runner comes in. Coach calls

time, and the ball is dead. The third-base runner is out, but the batter remains at bat. All other runners return to their previous bases.

Rule as Stated: 7.08 (h)

Any runner is out when passing a preceding runner before such runner is out. (p. 33)

Condensed Rule: There is never a good excuse for this occurrence. The rule states that one runner must never overtake another runner. The instant he passes him, he is out; the advanced runner is not out.

Hints and Tips: Simply warn all players.

Coach's Rules Drill: Put players on first and second bases. Hit deep hits in the two power alleys. Hit balls to the fences in left-center field and right-center field. Man on second should stay, but the runner from first should round second and pass the second-base runner on the way to third base; the man from first is called out, but not the runner originally on second.

Rule as Stated: 7.08 (i)

Any runner is out when, after acquiring legal possession of a base, he runs the bases in the reverse order, for the purpose of confusing the defense or of making a travesty or farce of the game. The umpire shall immediately call "Time" and call that runner out. Exception: If a runner touches an unoccupied base, or thinks the ball was caught or is decoyed before returning to the last base touched, runner may be put out running back to that base, but if runner reaches that last occupied base safely, he cannot be put out while in contact with that base. (p. 33)

Condensed Rule: Running bases in reverse order can be done only when hustling back to a base after a caught fly.

Hints and Tips: Simply warn players not to make a farce of the game.

Coach's Rules Drill: (a) Place runner on first base, and have him steal on the pitch. Hit a deep fly to center field. Runner, when getting to third, should suddenly reverse direction, touching second and first. Call him out. (b) Put runners on third base. Pitcher should take his stretch. Suddenly third-base runner heads for first, touching second and then first. Call him out.

Rule as Stated: 7.08 (j)

Any runner is out when failing to return at once to first base after overrunning or oversliding the base. If attempting to run to second, then runner is out when tagged. If, after overrunning or oversliding first base, runner starts toward the dugout, or towards his position, and fails to return to first base at once, then runner is out, on appeal, when he or the base is tagged. (p. 33)

Condensed Rule: The rule as stated seems obvious enough. Any time a runner is off base, he may be tagged out.

Hints and Tips: From first base, if runner turns toward the dugout, he can be tagged out.

Coach's Rules Drill: (a) Have runners run from home to first as coach hits grounders to the infield. After runner passes first base, he must turn in toward second. First baseman tags him. (b) Do the same drill as above, except have the runner head a few steps toward the bench. Yell "Safe!" First baseman then should run over and tag the runner or the base. Now the runner is out.

Rule as Stated: 7.08 (k)

Any runner is out when, in running or sliding for home base, runner fails to touch home base and makes no attempt to return to that base, if a fielder holds the ball in his hand while touching home base, and then appeals to the umpire for the decision. This applies only to the case where the runner who missed home plate is on the way to the dugout and the catcher would have to chase runner to tag out. It does not apply to the ordinary play where the player misses the plate and quickly tries to reach and retouch it before being tagged out. In this latter case, the runner must be tagged. (p. 33)

Condensed Rule: A runner who misses home plate and heads for the dugout is out if the catcher touches the plate with the ball.

Hints and Tips: To be sure, if player feels he might have missed home plate, he should reach back and touch it again before catcher can make the tag.

Coach's Rules Drill: (a) With a runner on third base, hit singles to left field. Runner should slide and miss home plate, then get up and go to the bench. Catcher touches the plate. Call the runner out. (b) With a runner on third base, hit singles to left field. Runner slides and misses the plate, but this time waits for the catcher to throw the ball to the pitcher. The runner then goes over and touches the plate. Call the runner safe.

Rule as Stated: 7.09 (a)

It is interference by a batter or a runner when, after a third strike, player hinders the catcher in his attempt to field the ball. The penalty for any kinds of interference is always that the runner is out and the ball is dead. The ball is dead at the time of interference and all runners go back to where they were at the time of interference. (p. 34)

Condensed Rule: None.

Hints and Tips: None.

Coach's Rules Drill: Pitcher should throw curves to the batter, who misses. On strike three, the catcher lets the ball pop out of his glove in front of the plate and toward first base. The batter then moves between the ball and catcher. The batter is called out, and the ball is dead. All other runners return to their bases.

Rule as Stated: 7.09 (b)

It is interference by a batter or a runner when, after hitting or bunting a fair ball, the bat hits the ball a second time in fair territory. The ball is dead and no runners may advance. If the batter-runner drops the bat in fair territory, and, in the umpire's judgment, there was no attempt to interfere with the course of the ball, then the ball is live and in play. (p. 34)

Condensed Rule: This is a rare accident, but difficult to avoid. The batter is called out and runners on base do not advance.

Hints and Tips: None.

Coach's Rules Drill: This rule is not practical for drill purposes; it is difficult to simulate.

Rule as Stated: 7.09 (c)

It is interference by a batter or a runner when intentionally deflecting the course of a foul ball in any manner. (p. 34)

Condensed Rule: The runner or batter may never intentionally touch a ball in or near foul territory.

Hints and Tips: Umpire must judge this as intentional.

Coach's Rules Drill: With a runner at the plate, drop a slow roller down the first-base line, as if it were a hit foul ball. Runner starts to first base and kicks the ball fair as he passes it. Call the runner out. The ball is dead. All other runners must go back to their previous bases.

Rule as Stated: 7.09 (d)

It is interference by a batter or a runner when, before two are out, and with a runner on third base, the batter hinders a fielder in making a play at home base. The runner is out, not the batter. (p. 34)

Condensed Rule: Batter cannot interfere with a play at home. If a runner is on third base, he is the out. The batter is not out.

Hints and Tips: Batter should step back on a play at home.

Coach's Rules Drill: Have the bases loaded. Coach should roll the ball slowly in front of the plate toward the pitcher as if it were a hit. The third-base runner is forced to come home. The batter then steps in front of the plate and blocks the catcher from getting to the plate. The runner is called out, but not the batter.

Rule as Stated: 7.09 (e)

It is interference by a batter or runner when any member of the offensive team stands or gathers around any base to which a runner is advancing, to confuse, hinder, or add to the difficulty of the fielders. Such runner shall be declared out for interference of those teammates. (p. 34)

Condensed Rule: None.

Hints and Tips: All team members should stay away from plays at the bases.

Coach's Rules Drill: Act as if the winning run is scoring. With a runner on second, coach should hit a single between left and center field. As the throw from the outfield and the second-base runner come toward the plate, have several players run out around plate on all sides. The runner attempting to score is out. All other runners go back to the last base they had held at the time of interference.

Rule as Stated: 7.09 (f)

It is interference by a batter or runner when any batter or runner who has just been put out hinders or impedes any following play being made on a runner. Such runner shall be declared out for the interference of the teammate. (p. 34)

Condensed Rule: One runner on a base may not assist or interfere with another teammate on a base.

Hints and Tips: When thrown or tagged out, get up and leave that base area immediately.

Coach's Rules Drill: With a player on first base, hit grounders to the second baseman in the baseline. Baseman tags the runner coming into him. That runner then gets in the way of the double-play throw to first base. Both runners are called out.

Rule as Stated: 7.09 (g)

It is interference by a batter or a runner when, if, in the judgment of the umpire, a base runner willfully and deliberately interferes with a batted ball or a fielder in the act of fielding a batted ball with the obvious intent to break up the double play, the ball is dead. The umpire shall call the runner out for interference and also call out the batter-runner because of the action of the teammate. This creates a double play to be committed. In no case may bases be run or runs scored because of such action from a runner. If ball is dead, all runners would have to go back to the original bases. (p. 34)

Condensed Rule: Runners must not impede the fielding or throwing of a ball on any play.

Hints and Tips: Runner must get out of the way of a hit ball and stay out of the line of a thrown ball.

Coach's Rules Drill: With players on first and second bases, hit a hard grounder to the shortstop over toward second base. Second-base runner should stay in the line of the shortstop's throw to second base. Both the interfering runner and the batter-runner are called out. Double play and a dead ball.

Rule as Stated: 7.09 (h)

It is interference by a batter or runner when, if, in the judgment of an umpire, a batter-runner willfully and deliberately interferes with a batted ball or a fielder in the act of fielding a batted ball, with the obvious intent to break up a double play, the ball is dead. The umpire shall call the batter-runner out for interference and shall also call out the runner who had advanced closest to home plate regardless of where the double play might have been possible. In no case shall bases be run because of such interference. (p. 34)

Condensed Rule: Batter-runners must not impede the fielding or throwing of a ball on any play.

Hints and Tips: The batter-runner must get out of the way of the hit ball and stay out of the line of a thrown ball.

Coach's Rules Drill: With the bases loaded, hit a hard grounder to first baseman on the first-base line. The batter runs in front of throw home to start a home-to-first double play. Call both the interfering batter-runner and the runner coming home out.

Rule as Stated: 7.09 (i)

It is interference by a batter or runner when, in the judgment of the umpire, the third base coach or first base coach, by touching or holding the runner, physically assists runner in returning to or leaving third base or first base. (p. 34)

Condensed Rule: Third- or first-base coach must never touch a runner.

Hints and Tips: The runner should not round third base so wide that he runs into the coaching box.

Coach's Rules Drill: (a) With players on first and second base, hit a slow grounder to the shortstop, who throws to first base. Second-base runner rounds third, grabs the third-base coach, and then dives to third base. He is not out! (b) Same situation as above. After bobbling the ball, the shortstop throws to third base; runner dives back to third with the

help of the third-base coach. The runner is called out.

Rule as Stated: 7.09 (j)

It is interference by a batter or runner when, with a runner on third base, that base coach leaves the box and acts in any manner to draw a throw by a fielder. (p. 34)

Condensed Rule: Third-base coach should stay in the box.

Hints and Tips: None.

Coach's Rules Drill: With a runner on second base, direct the pitcher to throw wild. The second-base runner goes on to third base. Third-base coach runs out on the third-base line, waving his arms and yelling "Third, third." Catcher then throws to third base, and the throw goes into left field. The third-base runner is called out.

Rule as Stated: 7.09 (k)

It is interference by a batter or a runner when, in running the last half of the distance from home base to first base while the ball is being fielded to first base, runs outside of (to the right of) the three foot line, or inside (to the left of) the foul line, and, in the umpire's judgment, interferes with the fielder taking the throw at first base, or attempting to field a batted ball. In such a rule, the runner is required to have both feet inside the "lane" between the chalk lines. (p. 34)

Condensed Rule: The runner from home to first must stay between chalk lines, except in making the turn.

Hints and Tips: Runner may knock down the fielder taking the throw if the fielder is in the chalk line path.

Coach's Rules Drill: With a runner at the plate, hit grounders to the infield. First runner runs inside the line and knocks baseman off base. Call the runner out. Next, station the baseman inside the line. As he reaches for the ball, the runner hits him. Again, the runner is out. Finally, station the fielder between the chalk lines. This time, when the runner hits baseman, the runner is safe.

Rule as Stated: 7.09 (l)

It is interference by a batter or runner when failing to avoid a fielder who is attempting to field a batted ball, or intentionally interferes with a ball that is thrown, provided that, if two or more fielders attempt to field a batted ball and the runner comes in contact with one or more of them, the umpire shall then determine which of the two fielders is entitled to the benefit of this rule. He shall not declare the runner is out for coming in contact with a fielder other than the one the umpire determines to be entitled to the ball. Note: When a catcher and the batter-runner come in contact as the runner is going to first base when the catcher is fielding the ball, there is generally no violation, and nothing should be called. (p. 35)

Condensed Rule: Runners must avoid contact with fielders.

Hints and Tips: Runners who stay between the two chalk lines going to first usually avoid a collision.

Coach's Rules Drill: Batter at the plate runs to first after laying down a slow roller halfway up to first base. Pitcher and first baseman both go to the ball on the line. Runner runs into both men on the way to first base. The runner is called out. It is possible to interfere with two fielders at the same time.

Rule as Stated: 7.09 (m)

It is interference by a batter or runner when touched by a fair ball in fair territory before touching a fielder. If a fair ball goes by or through an infielder and touches a runner immediately in back of him, or touches the runner after having been deflected by the fielder, the umpire shall not declare the runner out for having been touched by a batted ball. In making such decision, the umpire must decide that the ball is by or through the infielder who had a chance to make a play on the ball. If the ball went by an infielder, and the runner deliberately kicked or reached out to deflect such a ball, then the runner shall be called out for interference. (p. 35)

Condensed Rule: Do not let a fair fly or grounder touch you at any time. Runner must know that if touched by a fair ball hit *after* it passes the nearest

infielder, the ball is live. Runners advance as many bases as possible. But runners cannot kick such a ball intentionally.

Hints and Tips: If ball has touched or passed an infielder, the hit runner may advance any number of bases.

Coach's Rules Drill: Same drill as for 7.04 (b).

Rule as Stated: 7.10 (a)

Any runner shall be called out, only on appeal, if, after a fly ball, failing to touch his original base before either runner or the base is tagged. A runner is not permitted to take a "Flying Start" from several feet beyond the base. Runner must have at least one foot touching the base he leaves when the ball is caught. (p. 35)

Condensed Rule: Runners must tag up on a fly ball.

Hints and Tips: Runner should leave the bag the instant he sees ball disappear into the fielder's glove.

Coach's Rules Drill: Place runners on the three bases and hit deep flies to the outfielders. When the ball is hit, have the runners back up five feet behind each base. As the ball is caught, the runner should hit the bag with his foot, running toward the next base. Throw ball into that last base. As the baseman touches the bag, call the runner out.

Rule as Stated: 7.10 (b)

Any runner shall be called out, only on appeal, if, with the ball in play, while advancing or returning to a base, runner fails to touch each base in order before runner, or a missed base, is tagged. (p. 35)

Condensed Rule: Touching and retouching bases must be done in order.

Hints and Tips: Avoid this by knowing the correct number of outs.

Coach's Rules Drill: Same drill as for 7.08 (d).

Rule as Stated: 7.10 (c)

Any runner shall be called out, only on appeal, if runner overruns or overslides first base and fails to return to the base immediately, and runner or the base is tagged. (p. 35)

Condensed Rule: Must return immediately. Runner who has crossed first base and goes beyond it in running or sliding must return to that base immediately, and he must do it in a straight path.

Hints and Tips: Return to first base straight down the line.

Coach's Rules Drill: Same drill as for 7.08 (c).

Rule as Stated: 7.10 (d)

Any runner shall be called out, only on appeal, if runner fails to touch home base and makes no attempt to return to that base, then home base is tagged. Any appeal on this play must be made before the next pitch or before the next play. (p. 35)

Condensed Rule: Catcher touches home plate with the ball. Runner is out. Runner who feels that he may have missed home plate on a slide or a run might immediately touch home plate. Runner who missed home plate will be safe, unless the defense appeals and touches the plate.

Hints and Tips: If the catcher missed seeing runner tag home, or missed tagging home plate, runner goes and sits down quickly on the bench.

Coach's Rules Drill: Same drill as for 7.08 (k).

Rule as Stated: 7.11

All players, coaches, or any member of an offensive team shall vacate any space on the field (including both dugouts) needed by a fielder who is attempting to field a batted or thrown ball. The penalty for this shall be that interference shall be called and the batter or the runner on whom the play is made, shall be declared out. (p. 36)

Condensed Rule: All players in dugouts or sidelines must move out of the way.

Hints and Tips: None.

Coach's Rules Drill: This is not a practical situation for a drill because the incidence is very low.

Rule as Stated: 7.12

Unless two are out, the status of a following runner is not affected by a preceding runner's failure to touch or retouch a base. If upon appeal, the preceding runner is the third out, no runners following him shall score. If such third out is the result of a force play, neither preceding nor following runners shall score. (p. 36)

Condensed Rule: None.

Hints and Tips: None.

Coach's Rules Drill: With runners on first and second bases, hit a deep hit through the power alley. Both runners score. The second-base runner fails to touch third base. The first-base runner touches all bases. The defense executes an appeal play at third base. Second-base runner is called out, but the first-base runner still scores.

Section 8.05: The Pitcher's Balk

Each runner must look for and be able to argue ''balk'' with any umpire. After all, it is the runner who is jeopardized if it is not called correctly. It is the runner who benefits if it is called correctly. Quoted from *Official Baseball Rules*, there are 13 types of balks a pitcher may commit. If he commits any one of these balks, each runner on the bases, but not the batter, is awarded his next base. The 13 balk situations are as follows:

1. *The pitcher, while touching the rubber, makes any motion naturally associated with his pitches and fails to deliver the ball.*
2. *The pitcher, while touching the rubber, feigns a throw to first base and fails to complete the throw there.*
3. *The pitcher, while touching the rubber, fails to step directly toward a base before throwing to that base.*
4. *The pitcher, while touching the rubber, throws, or feigns a throw to an unoccupied base, except for the purpose of making a play.*
5. *The pitcher makes an illegal pitch.*
6. *The pitcher delivers the ball to a batter while not facing the batter.*

7. *The pitcher makes any motion naturally associated with his pitch, while not touching the rubber.*
8. *The pitcher unnecessarily delays the game.*
9. *The pitcher, without having the ball, stands on, or astride, the pitcher's rubber or, while off the plate, he feigns a pitch.*
10. *The pitcher, after coming to a legal pitching position, removes one hand from the ball other than in an actual pitch, or in throwing to a base.*
11. *The pitcher, while touching the rubber, accidentally or intentionally drops the ball.*
12. *The pitcher, while giving a batter an intentional walk, pitches while the catcher is not in the catcher's box.*
13. *The pitcher delivers from the "set position" without first coming to a stop. (pp. 39-40)*

Runners should remember that if the opposing pitcher commits any one of the 13 balks listed above, they should be awarded a base. A balk should be called by the umpire. Runners should always wait until the umpire signals them to advance to the next base.

Section 10.08: When Is a Base Stolen?

The following list carefully defines what is and is not a stolen base. Many baseball players believe that any time a player advances safely from one base to another, he has stolen a base. Not true! The list is based upon Section 10.08, "The Rules of Scoring." *Of nine situations occurring in baseball, only three of the nine situations would be correctly scored as a stolen base.* Scorekeepers, official scorers, and coaches often record these as cheap stolen bases, and they are not at all. Make a runner earn his official stolen base.

The base runner is credited with a stolen base in these situations:

1. Runner starts to steal before the delivery, and a wild pitch results or a passed ball results.
2. Runner steals and catcher throws wildly to that next base.
3. Runner evades a rundown or pickoff try and advances to the next base.
4. Runner is a part of a double or triple steal,

and the advance runner is safe. Here, all runners get credited with stolen bases. If the advance runner is out, no other runner gets a stolen base.

The base runner is *not* credited with a stolen base in these situations:

1. Runner overslides a base and is tagged out after successfully stealing.
2. Runner is out, but baseman drops the ball, or it is kicked loose from his glove.
3. Runner steals, but the defense is indifferent to him and allows him to steal.
4. Infielder drops the ball or mishandles it.

The Infield Fly Rule

As quoted from *Official Baseball Rules*, the infield fly is described as follows:

An "infield fly" is a fair ball (which does not include a line drive or an attempted bunt), which can be caught by an infielder with ordinary effort when runners are only on the following combinations of bases: (a) Men on first and second bases; or (b) Bases loaded. The "infield fly" rule does not apply if two are out (only if there are none or one away). The pitcher, catcher, or any of the other four infielders shall be considered infielders for the purpose of this rule. When it is quite apparent that the batted ball will become an "INFIELD FLY" in accordance with all of the above, the umpire shall immediately yell LOUDLY, "INFIELD FLY" for the benefit of the runners on the bases. If the "INFIELD FLY" is near the foul line, the umpire shall yell "INFIELD FLY, IF FAIR." (p. 8)

The ball is alive, and men on base must be very alert. Runners may advance at the risk of the ball being caught, or they may retouch their bases and advance after the catch, the same as with any fly ball. If the hit ball is foul, it is treated as any foul ball and is no longer an infield fly. If the fly ball is dropped and bounces foul before it reaches first or third bases, it is a foul ball, not an infield fly. If the fly ball is dropped in foul territory and bounces fair before it reaches first or third bases, it is an infield fly. If a fair infield fly ball is dropped intentionally by an infielder, the batter is out automatically. All runners advance at their own peril.

If the infield fly is caught or drops at the feet of the infielder so he can retrieve it quickly, stay on your base. Do not move! If it drops and rolls away from the infielder, run to the next base. If it is dropped at his feet or hits his glove, and he lets it dribble out, remember that he may be doing this intentionally! This rule was revised to protect the runner from an automatic double play. Do not fall for this trap. This play occurs quite often. But if the runner gets caught off base and run down, he is caught in a trap often laid by the defense when the infield fly occurs.

The First- and Third-Base Coach

In this special section, I wish to warn all runners and base coaches concerning the limits of coaches in assisting runners. The degree to which coaches may assist is specifically outlined in *Official Baseball Rules*, under Sections 7.0 to 7.12.

While the runner is rounding first or third base, be certain that the runner and the base coach do not touch each other. If the runner takes a wide turn, be certain that the runner does not run into the base coach. The umpire will call the runner out for assisting the runner. Even if the touching is accidental, runners can be called out. If the runner slips and falls, the coach must make no move to help him. However, a base coach may touch the runner if no play is under way on that part of the diamond and if no play involves that runner. This ruling is found in Section 7.09 (i). Coaches may help runners vocally and at any time yell instructions, but coaches may never assist them physically, or even touch them, during a play.

Base coaches may call time out as many times as they wish during a ball game, unless the umpire feels that they are unnecessarily delaying the game. When base coaches call time out, be sure the umpire makes that call. The runner may step off the base and go to the base coach's box and talk, or he may have the base coach come to the base where the runner is standing. But it is better to have the runner leave the base and go to the coach's box, so the conversation will not be overheard by the first or third baseman. When the ball is in play the first- and third-base coaches must stay in their coach's boxes. They may come down the box,

parallel to the baseline as far as the chalk line extends, but they should not cross the chalk line parallel to the baseline. If they do, the umpire will warn them a time or two, and if they do not heed the warning, he can remove them from the game.

When coaching first or third base, there is an inherent danger of being hit by line drives. Be alert; these drives are hit with tremendous velocity. The maximum speed of a pitched ball is around 100 mph; the batted ball travels even faster. Unalert base coaches have sustained serious injuries from hard drives. If a coach cannot get completely out of the path of a drive ball, he should try to make the ball hit him with a glancing blow. This will usually minimize serious injury. Be especially aware of which batters on the squad are ''pull'' hitters, the ones who often hit this type of hard drive.

Be certain coaches quickly and fully vacate the coach's box if a fly is to be caught near them or if a fielder comes over to field a hit ball or wild throw. Coaches must quickly react and make every reasonable effort to vacate that area. If they don't, the umpire will not hesitate to call the batter out. Umpires will usually give the defense the benefit of the doubt.

The best assistance base coaches can give runners includes (a) encouragement in everything said and done, (b) knowledge of the rules of running, and (c) immediate conference with the umpires after a play if the coach feels that either judgment or rules calls have been improper. The coach should defend the runner immediately, if he feels he is right. Let all runners know that you are their defender and are not afraid to stand up for them.

The Appeal Plays

Appeal plays are common in baseball but often misunderstood by coaches and players alike. To aid understanding of those plays that can be appealed and how to appeal them, I have divided the appeal plays into offensive and defensive appeals. Each situation is taken from *Official Baseball Rules* and discussed thoroughly.

Offensive Appeal Plays

- Appeal to the plate umpire for a catcher not tagging the batter or throwing to first base when a "trapped third strike" occurs. Also appeal to the umpire to advance runners to their next bases. Appeal plays are requested by the offense only in the case of probable error in the interpretation of rules—not in the case of judgment calls. Teams are not allowed to appeal a judgment call.

- If the umpire ignores or refuses to reverse a decision on the basis of a team's appeal and the team feels certain a rule has been misinterpreted, the team may at that point announce to the umpire that it is playing the game under protest. After the game is over, and if they are the loser, the appealing team may appeal the call to the chief of umpires in the area or to league officials. The chief will study the appeal request, and if the appealing team is allowed the decision, the game will be played over from that point of play. If the appealing team won the game, they should go to the umpire after the game and declare that they are withdrawing the protest.

Defensive Appeal Plays

- Appeal to the plate umpire for a batter not checking his swing or for swinging around. If the base umpire nods and calls it a strike, then the ball called by the plate umpire is overruled. The plate umpire requests the call.

- Appeal to the umpire nearest a base for a base runner failing to touch that base. If your pitcher goes into his stretch position, steps off the mound, and tosses the ball to a baseman touching that base, then the umpire will signal safe or out for the runner who just passed.

- Appeal to the umpire nearest that base for a base runner not tagging up on a caught fly. If your pitcher goes into his stretch position, steps off the mound, and tosses the ball to the baseman touching that base, then the umpire will signal safe or out for the runner who just passed.

- Appeal to the umpire nearest that base if the runner fails to return to that base after a foul ball hit by the batter. Throw the ball back to the pitcher, who takes his stretch, steps off the mound and throws to an infielder covering that base.

- Appeal to the plate umpire for a batter who has batted out of turn. Ask the umpire to check with the official scorekeeper. If it is true that the batter has batted out of turn, he will be called out by the umpire. This appeal must be made by the opponent before one pitch is thrown to the following batter.

- Appeal to the umpire nearest that base for a runner who missed a base to return and retouch all bases in reverse order. If the runner failed to come back and retouch the bases in reverse order, an appeal to the nearest base umpire governs this case. The pitcher must throw the ball to a baseman touching that base before delivering the first pitch to the batter.

- Appeal to the plate umpire for a runner missing home plate and not returning to touch it. Make the appeal and touch home plate with the foot while holding the ball. Umpire will call the runner safe or out.

- Appeal to the plate umpire for a runner coming in to score but failing to cross home plate before an out is made elsewhere against his team for the third out of the inning. Although it is a judgment call as to whether the foot touched the plate before the out was made somewhere else on the bases, the coach appeals to the plate umpire. The umpire will allow or disallow the run.

The rules of running may seem, on the theoretical level, too complex for the young player to master. But in practice, they are learned easily because team members can see the applications in drills and then follow through in actual games. And most players learn quickly when they discover how much fun it is to execute the plays.

Now I would like to take you for a guided tour around the bases—a distance greater than it might seem.

Chapter

4

A Grand Tour
of the Bases

From base to base, the journey around the diamond is only 120 yards, or 360 feet. Yet it is often a long trip, one that includes a great many surprise events and novel sights for the traveler and the spectator as well. In this chapter I will act as tour guide. Starting from home plate, we will travel slowly, stopping to examine each possible event at every point of interest to the runner. This discussion will be continued in chapter 5, where more specific base-stealing mechanics will be covered.

The grand tour will be divided into four parts: (a) home plate to first base, (b) first base to second base, (c) second base to third base, and (d) third base to home plate. After we arrive back home, I'll give a concluding talk on some key defensive points as well as tips on how to run bases on fly balls near foul lines, run when trapped between bases, protect yourself against the hidden-ball trick, run on a pop-up behind the catcher, slide properly, and score the first run of a game.

Portions of the material on pp. 89-91 were adapted from *Sports Illustrated BASEBALL*, © 1983 Time Inc., by Jerry Kindall. Used with permission.

Tour 1: Running From Home Plate to First Base

Since this is the run all players will execute most often, it is the one they should practice hardest and know best. When they head for first base, they are forced to go there; they have no choice.

All of baserunning is grounded on three basic skills:

- The first step—initial acceleration
- The run—the player's running form and natural speed
- The approach to the base—a slide or step to the base

The First Step

After the batter hits the ball, he lets the upper body follow through in the swing and discards the bat immediately. If he batted from the right side, his first step should be a driving push-off taken with the rear (right) foot toward first base. If the batter is left-handed, the first step after the swing is with the rear (left) foot. Whether left- or right-handed, batters commonly make the mistake of taking that first step toward the pitcher's mound or toward the first-base dugout. Since a batter is running toward first base, he should do so from the very first step! The first several strides should be short and choppy, with the body somewhat low to pick up momentum as quickly as possible. After three or four steps, the runner should be in full stride and going at maximum speed.

To determine whether a runner should run straight to the bag or swing out to the right and make the turn at first base, he must know if the ball will be fielded in the infield, so he looks briefly to the left once full speed has been reached. If the ball appears likely to be fielded, the runner must, of course, try to beat the infielder's throw, so he turns both eyes back to the bag. On a close throw, a runner's inclination is often to take a long, desperate leap at the bag from 10 or 12 feet away. This is a big mistake. The runner finds that he will reach the bag far more quickly if a long, floating leap is turned into two quick strides across the bag. Runners lose momentum when they launch into the air like a bird, whereas they maintain or even gain momentum with an additional stride. If an umpire's last visual impression is of a runner floating through the air as the ball nears the first baseman's glove, the call will likely be ''out!''

In general, when running to first base, the runner tries to make himself run 95 feet through the bag, not 90 feet to it. This will eliminate any tendency to slow down near the bag. The runner should hit the front of the bag with either foot and as the next stride carries him over the bag, glance quickly over his right shoulder to see if the throw has gotten past the first baseman. If it has and the ball has rolled far enough, the runner knows immediately, without the first-base coach telling him, that he can advance to second base. If the runner is safe, and the first baseman catches the ball, the runner should regain control quickly, return to the bag, and watch for a possible bad throw from the first baseman to the pitcher.

The only time it is proper to slide into first base is to avoid a tag. If a runner sees the first baseman's foot coming off the bag to catch a high or wide throw, then he should slide either feetfirst or headfirst to avoid the first baseman's sweeping tag. Tag plays at first base happen more often than a runner thinks, but if a runner watches that first baseman's foot he can avoid them and raise his on-base percentage another notch.

The first step or initial acceleration is most important; it spells success or defeat when a runner arrives at the next base. A good runner should work on perfecting his first step away from the plate, constantly decreasing the time it takes him to get out of the batter's box.

Figure 4.1 The run from home to first: After three or four steps, the runner should be in full stride, going at maximum speed.

The Run

Recent evidence has shown that with proper training running speed can indeed be enhanced. In addition, improvements in running speed can be realized by refining the initial step, the slide, and other factors of the run such as alertness, swift thinking, daring, and the ability to challenge and intimidate the defense. Often a player's aggressiveness, lack of fear, and willingness to slide and contact a defensive man will make up for a lack of speed. But a runner must know how fast he is and neither overestimate nor underestimate his relative speed.

Regardless of a player's inherent speed, he must learn proper running form in order to maximize his potential as a base stealer. Jerry Kindall, head coach at the University of Arizona, has outlined the elements of good running form in several published articles. The section to follow is a summary of his careful analysis. Coach Kindall stresses the importance of good technique, pointing out that a swimming coach would never tell his team merely to go for it, to "just get from one end of the pool to the other as fast as you can." Similarly, a base runner cannot merely thrash his way around the diamond and hope to beat the throw or the tag.

Effective running requires proper technique in every part of the body—literally from head to toe.

Run with the head up, eyes on the target, and a loose chin. When a runner grits his teeth and tightens his jaw, that tension transfers down the neck into the shoulders and restricts necessary shoulder work. Do not bob the head up and down, or from side to side, diverting it in any way from a straight line toward the target.

Run with the shoulders level and allow the arms to pump freely straight ahead, swinging out, down, and back from the shoulder. The arms act as pistons that drive the upper body straight ahead and should form approximately a 90-degree angle at the elbow. As the arms pump rapidly, the elbows should remain close to the sides to prevent the arms from flapping. As the arms pump forward, the hands should go no higher than the shoulders; if the hands proceed up past the shoulders, part of the momentum generated by the arms is dissipated upward rather than continued forward.

As the arms pump backward, the hands should go no farther than the hips before they begin their forward thrust. Both hands should be loosely cupped rather than tightly clenched. This prevents tension and tightness from being transferred up the arms to the shoulders and upper body. All action should be directed forward, not sideways, so that the upper body doesn't zigzag.

The faster and more efficiently the arms pump, the more the legs will do the same. The hips should be level throughout the running action. Keep the knees bent and lift them high—up to the level of the hips. Then extend each lower leg as far as possible toward the target. By lifting the knees high, a runner can lengthen the stride and cover more ground. The legs should not leap and glide, but rise, stretch, and thrust forward powerfully.

A runner should land on the ball of the foot, and the toes should be pointing straight ahead or slightly in with each stride. The best way to place the feet is along a straight line toward the target. A runner can practice foot placement by running up and down the baseline. Run with the left foot on the left of the line and your right foot on the right of the line. The body should be leaning forward about 18 to 20 degrees as the runner begins stretching the lead leg into its stride.

Figure 4.2 Proper running form.

The Approach to the Base

The third skill, the approach to the base, is perfected through constant practice. When reaching first base, the good runner will run across the bag down the line toward right field, rounding the bag and taking a wide turn to head for second base. Or he may choose to slide into first base on a close play. Sliding into first when coming from home is not practiced by many runners and its use should be limited as discussed previously.

In practice, the runner must make himself do all these things daily, for he may have to use all of them in each game. Here are all the playing situations that might affect a runner's decision on the way from home to first base:

- Grounder to an infielder
- Fly ball to an infielder
- Base hit to an outfielder
- Fly ball to an outfielder
- Bunted ball
- Run to first base after a missed third strike by catcher

For each situation, simple instructions should be given to the runner.

Grounder to an Infielder.   Get a fast initial step and run to first base as hard as possible on every hit ball. Assume that the fielder will make an error; never give up. Always run between the two white chalk lines. When the runner reaches first base, he should cross the bag fast. If the first baseman has failed to stop the throw from the infielder, the runner should turn toward the diamond and make a beeline for second base if the ball has gone a considerable distance. If it is still nearby, the runner should go back to first base and wait.

Fly Ball to an Infielder.   Always assume that the infielder will drop the ball. If a runner hustles hard and an infielder drops a high pop-up, the runner should make it to second base on the error.

Base Hit to an Outfielder.   Get that fast initial step, run hard to first base, and round the base correctly, stepping on the inside of the base with the right foot. Take a wide turn toward second base. The deeper the hit, the wider the turn and the closer to second base he can go before stopping. Hustle back to first base as the throw from the outfield is relayed back to the infield. The runner should al-

ways be a maximum distance off first base so he can break for second in case the ball is bobbled by the outfielder.

Fly Ball to an Outfielder.   Always assume that every fly ball will be dropped in the outfield. If a player hits a short or medium fly ball to an outfielder who drops it, by the time the fielder gets it in his glove the runner should be halfway between first and second base. If not, he hasn't hustled. If the fielder drops the ball, second base is assured. If the batter hits a long fly to the outfield or hits between two outfielders, he should be running near second base by the time it is caught. If the ball is dropped, the runner can easily make it to third base if the ball rolls away from the outfielder. Base runners often loaf when they hit long flies and watch the ball too much.

A Bunted Ball.   The initial step is of prime importance on this play. After the hitter feels the bat hit the ball, he should run very hard down the line to first base, cross the bag, and hope for an overthrow at first. If the overthrow occurs, he should easily be able to make the turn and slide safely into second base.

Running to First Base After a Missed Third Strike by Catcher.   This is a common weakness on the part of all hitters. After the hitter strikes out, he often is so angry with himself he forgets to see if the third strike was caught. Always assume that it will not be caught, especially if it is a low ball in the dirt or a breaking curveball. The first reaction when a hitter strikes out must be to run. Do it instinctively! If there is a question as to whether the ball is caught, he should run to first base, then settle the question later. The rule states that if the third strike is not caught, the catcher must tag the batter with the ball or throw to first base for the out. Never stand at the plate and allow the catcher to make the tag. If a batter runs to first base, the catcher may make a bad throw, and the runner will end up on second base instead of sitting on the bench.

What else could happen to a batter after he hits the ball and heads for first base? Believe it or not, there have been rundown plays between home and first. The first baseman fields the ball on the line about 20 feet in toward home plate. Instead of going to first base and touching the bag, he goes out to touch the runner. But the panicked runner stops and starts back toward home. The first baseman and catcher then start a rundown. Once or twice in Little League I've seen the ball thrown past the catcher's ear, all the way to the backstop, with the runner ending up on second base. More likely, though, he will be tagged out. These green runners and defensive players all forgot that first is the only base the runner may only run toward. On any other play, a runner may retreat to the original base.

When running from home to first base after hitting a high pop-up that a pitcher, catcher, or first baseman may try to field, the batter should run down the line between the chalk lines. That is his right-of-way. If, however, the infielder needs to catch the ball in that area between the two lines, the runner must go around him to first base. He can't bump, touch, or in any way interfere with the fielder attempting to catch the ball. If he does, he will be called out on runner interference. Here again, the key to good running is hustle; always assume the fielder will make an error and you will increase the odds for arriving safely at the next base. Positive thinking and hard running reinforce each other and make the effort pay off.

Tour 2: Running From First Base to Second Base

A runner on first base is automatically forced to run toward second base when a fly or grounder is hit. The runner must always run on a grounder and must vacate first base if a fly is hit. Obviously, the hitter would have nowhere to go if the first-base runner does not break. If the fly is caught, the runner comes back to first base, of course, and the hitter is out.

Any first-base runner must know the following:

- What to do if a grounder is hit
- What to do if a line drive fly is hit
- What to do if a short, medium, or deep fly is hit
- What to do on a pickoff attempt
- What sign is being given. Know the play coming up
- The score (the most important item)
- The number of outs
- The count
- Where the batter at the plate usually hits
- The inning
- Who has the ball now

The most important helper at this point on the bases is the first-base coach. He is a specialist trained to get the runner on his way safely.

How to Coach First Base

When a double, triple, home run, or deep fly is hit, and the runner steams around first base, the coach's responsibility is to yell "Take two, take two" if it's a sure double, "Go for three, go for three" if it's a sure triple, or "Don't loaf—hustle—get going" if it's a home run. Don't let the runner slow down, even on a sure home run, and make sure he hits the base. Watch the foot touch in case the play at the bag is appealed. But once a player reaches second base and heads for third, the runner then becomes the responsibility of the third-base coach.

The first-base coach should first ask the runner the score and the inning and correct him if he's wrong. Also ask the runner the number of outs. A runner on base who doesn't know these three facts is dangerous to himself and the team. Next say, "You have to go on a grounder," followed by, "Go way down on a deep fly" and "Go one third of the way on a short fly." If the team is ahead by a few runs, say, "I want you on third base on a single." The runner should be daring, but sensible. If there are two outs, yell, "You have to go on anything hit." The last thing to say before the pitch is "Break up the double play." This will be the last thing he hears before he runs.

If the count is three-and-two with two outs, remind the runner he must go on the pitch and watch for a pickoff on all bases! Remind him this is a favorite time for pickoff throws. Of course, the first-base coach also helps the first-base runner get the sign. Both coach and runner must know the sign and the upcoming play. In a close ball game, the coach must be sure to remind the runner when he arrives at first whether he represents the tying or winning run. The first-base coach may have a mechanical counter in his hand. He should keep the count of balls and strikes and always remind the runner of the count after each pitch.

A first-base coach must always be alert for a pickoff throw from the catcher or pitcher. He should yell loudly, "Get back" or "dive" on each pickoff try and remind the runner not to be leaning toward the next base. The coach should also remind the runner on which pitches the pickoff may be attempted. The runner needs to be prodded to take a maximum lead. The coach should always call time out if the runner doesn't understand his instructions, and have a conference with the runner before resuming play. But before any of this, both must know *who has the baseball*. (See "The Hidden-Ball Trick" later in this chapter for more information.)

All this may seem like a lot for the runner to know and do. A baseball game moves slowly, however, and each of these instructions can be given and understood before the next play. But the moment the runner leaves first base and heads for second, the only help a coach can give him on a hit ball is to shout instructions: "Slide," if a grounder is hit to an infielder; "Break up the double play," on a grounder; and "Get back, get back," if runner foolishly goes on a fly, forgetting the number of outs. Be sure the runner comes back and tags first base after either foul balls or caught flies.

Defensive Plays Against First-Base Runners

There are two plays that the defense can use to fool first-base runners. Beware of these, especially when the opposition is trailing and desperate. "Getting a Double Play on a Bunt Attempt" and the "Whip" are plays that outfielders, the relay man, and the first baseman practice to catch first-base runners off guard.

In the double play on a bunt attempt, the batter lays down his bunt, and the first-base runner stands up at second base and does not slide. The throw goes to first base for one out. Usually, the second baseman is covering first base on the throw. He then fires the ball to the shortstop covering second base, to try to catch the runner leaning toward third base. Often the runner can't get back and is tagged out. Now, instead of a man on second base in scoring position, the running team has no one on base and two outs.

In the whip play, the batter hits a single to any outfield, and takes a big round turn at first base. As the ball comes in to the shortstop or the second baseman, the hitter lazily retreats back toward first base. He may also make the mistake of sometimes turning his back on the ball. Instead of the shortstop or second baseman lobbing the ball to the pitcher on the mound, he will quickly whip the ball to the first baseman, who puts the tag on the unsuspecting runner.

Hard Singles to Right Field

Often a hitter singles sharply to a right fielder. The ball arrives very quickly to the right fielder, who is usually playing up and over toward left field for a right-handed hitter. The fielder really isn't very far from either first or second base. The batter feels great getting that base hit. While he is congratulating himself on being such a good hitter, the right fielder, instead of relaying the ball to the second baseman, fires the ball to the first baseman standing on the bag. The great hitter is out.

He loafed down the baseline and perhaps didn't keep his eye on the hit ball. Such a play is not extremely rare. In one season, my right fielder worked on this play with the first baseman and pulled it twice. All batters should be cautioned to run hard on any hit and to keep an eye on the ball. A final warning to hitters should be to watch for this same play by a trailing catcher covering first base. The catcher may run down the first base line and sneak in behind first base to take the throw.

How to Break Up a Double Play at Second Base

This is one of the most important offensive plays in baseball. All players, up and down the lineup, must master this. Practice it daily. It is used whenever a runner has occasion to run from first to second base on a ground ball to an infielder. There is no faster way to be taken out of a game than to have double plays executed against you. The first and most important element of this play is the maximum lead. The runner will not be effective in this maneuver unless he has both speed and a big lead. The initial crossover step has to be fast. The runner should now head directly at second base.

The Shortstop Covers. When the runner gets to the point down the line where he begins his slide, he must remember to use the stand-up slide. He is not down trying to elude a tag, for this is not a tag play. It is a force play. The runner wants his entire body in front of the infielder covering second base because he wants to prevent the second baseman from relaying to first base for the double play. In a sense, this is the only obstruction or interference play allowed the running team. Section 7.08 (b) of *Official Baseball Rules* requires the runner to go straight into second base. This was probably passed to reduce the number of injuries occurring from this play.

At the point of takeoff on the slide, the runner must remember on which side of the field the grounder was hit. When the shortstop covers, the runner comes in from the left side, sliding to the left side of the bag. This will present the fielder with an obstruction; he must now throw, on the run—on the fly, so to speak—over the runner's body. Even for an experienced shortstop with a great arm, this is a very difficult throw on which to maintain concentration, accuracy, and speed. After the shortstop has released the ball, the runner should stay on second base until he learns from the umpire whether the man covering second base missed touching the base. The runner should ask the umpire if he is safe or not before leaving the second-base area for the dugout. He does not leave second base until he knows for sure he is out. After a runner slides, he should get up instantly, ready to go on to third base in case of an overthrow at first base.

The Second Baseman Covers. Follow the instructions given in the preceding section under "How to Break Up a Double Play at Second Base." At the point where the runner takes off in his slide, he must again remember to which side of the infield the ball was hit. In this case, it was grounded to an infielder on the left side. Again, Section 7.08 (b) requires the runner to go straight into second base. The runner is called out if he purposely brings his body up from sliding position and prevents the baseman from relaying the throw to first base. This rule applies only to lower levels of baseball, such as high school, American Legion, and so forth. The second baseman covers the bag and takes the throw. He will step on the right front corner of the bag. Remember, he will have less momentum on his throw to first base than would the shortstop. The second baseman must throw better and harder because he must throw more with his arm than with his entire body.

Therefore, the runner should slide to the right side of second base and come up touching the right corner. Just as the second baseman receives the ball, he must release it over the runner's body, which is coming up. This is very difficult for a young player to do without greatly reducing the velocity of the ball. Again, after the relay has gone to first

base, the runner should stay on second base to see if umpire called him out or safe, and he should be prepared to go to third base fast if he is safe and the ball is overthrown at first base.

How to Return to First Base on a Pickoff Attempt

The surest way to return to first base is to dive head-first. That will get the hand on the bag the fastest. If a runner feels he has taken too much lead, leaned too far toward second base, or has just been fooled, he should dive low for the outside (the right-field corner) of the bag. After touching it, he should not take his hand off the bag until the ball is thrown back to the pitcher. Many first basemen will fake a toss back to the pitcher, then quickly reach down and touch a runner as he gets up. But if the runner has time to stay on his feet and safely return to first base on the pickoff attempt, he should step toward the right-field corner of the bag, plant his left foot there, then swing his body clockwise around, away from the pitcher. This way, the runner stays behind the bag and eludes the tag of the first baseman. As the runner pivots toward right field, the first baseman must try to tag a moving body.

Tour 3: Running From Second to Third Base

The runner has now made it to second base, halfway home—he is now in scoring position because from this bag the average runner can score on a single, double, triple, home run, or even a bad error or a two-base suicide squeeze. In some cases, even a passed ball by the catcher could score a runner from second base, if the backstop is deep.

As soon as the runner lands safely on second base, he must realize three facts: (a) At second base, he may be picked off by either of two infielders; (b) he can take a much bigger lead off second than off first base; and (c) he is the "property" of the third-base coach and must watch and listen to him. The coach can help him score that run.

The second-base runner must always know what to do on a long, medium, or short fly, a line drive at an infielder, a bunt, a grounder to left or right side of infield, or a single to the outfield. He should watch for several types of tricky pickoff plays by the shortstop and/or the second baseman. Remember, the runner is not forced unless another runner is on first base. This is a favorite base for defensive teams attempting pickoff plays, especially if the teams are losing or desperate for an out. The types of pickoff plays are far too many to enumerate here. The second-base runner must constantly be on guard.

The best protection against pickoffs is the third-base coach. He will usually watch the shortstop because the runner's back is to that infielder. But the runner faces the second baseman and assumes responsibility for the latter. As he takes his lead, the runner must listen to the third-base coach at all times. The coach will announce if the shortstop is creeping in behind the runner.

Important Rules in Running Second Base

Tag up on deep, medium, and short flies. This is the base where the rule is always *tag up*. Don't ever lead off on a fly ball. After the catch, runner advances to third base only if he has the necessary speed.

When a grounder is hit hard to the left side of the infield, do not immediately advance. Hold a short lead. The runner may want to try for third base when the ball is being thrown to first base for the out. Running 75 feet to third base, the player must beat two throws, one of about 110 feet and one of 126 feet. If he has any speed at all, he should slide in safely on a close play.

When a grounder is hit to the right side of the infield, advance hard to third base if it is a weak or fairly weak hit. The runner should be safe at third base on a fielder's choice. If it is a hard grounder, do not move toward third base at all on the play. The runner surely will be thrown out, first to third base or on a tag play, fielder's choice. When a line drive is hit, dive back to second base to prevent being doubled off. The runner must react instantly to this situation.

When a ball is bunted softly and third base is unoccupied, the runner should break hard for third. If he gets the jump, no fielder can throw the runner out at third base on this play. If the runner doesn't have to slide, he should round third quickly and be ready to score on any throwing error to first.

When a suicide squeeze or two-base suicide is called for, runners on second and third must be

stealing on the pitch or they won't make it. The runner on second must get a big lead, watch closely for a pickoff, then break hard. He should be on third base by the time the ball is picked up by an infielder. As the fielder throws the ball to first base to get the bunter out, the runner should round third base and keep going. By the time the first baseman gets the throw, the runner should be about halfway home and win his foot race with the ball. It is always a close play, but the runner should always win.

On a single, when an outfielder fields a ground ball he must look down and take his eyes off the runner. He doesn't know how far the runner has gone. Depending on how the ball has been hit, the runner from second base should either stop at third or try to score. The third-base coach will make this decision, based on the runner's speed. The runner should slide hard into home, if told to do so. When a ball is hit to the outfield, go hard as soon as it is muffed or goes through. Runner will get to third base for sure and may score if the error is a bad one.

Finally, remember that when a runner scores, he should get right up, step back of the plate in line with third base, and be ready to signal the next runner coming in to stand or slide. He should use two hand signals: hands up to stand, or both hands pointing down to slide.

Tour 4: Running From Third Base to Home Plate

We have gone safely past many perils, all the way from home to third base. Now comes the hard part. The distance from third base to home plate is run less often than any of the others for the simple reason that fewer runners get that far. Remember, the only thing that really counts is how many runners cross home plate, and that makes the trip from third base to home most important of all. Defenses, of course, are geared more to preventing home from being gained because it is the one goal that really matters in baseball.

The third-base runner must know what to do when the batter hits a long, a medium, or a short fly and what to do on a hard or a slow grounder and on a bunt. He must always stay alert for the passed ball or wild pitch and watch closely for catcher and pitcher pickoffs. He must know the score, the inning, the number of outs, and remember to tag up on all fly balls. In addition, he must know how to run down and back the third-base line, one of the weakest skills for most ball players. Runners must hustle down the line as far as they can on each pitch, going only as far as they can to still get back on base in a fast dive. Anything less than this is not good enough.

If a runner hustles like this, he will score on a bunt that is hard to field; a slow roller; a grounder to the second-base area; a passed ball or a wild pitch; a base hit that goes over or through the infield; or a suicide or safe-squeeze bunt. A runner will score in each of these situations only if he has hustled the maximum distance from third base, leaving only 60 or 70 feet to slide across the plate safely, instead of 80 or 90 feet.

The third-base runner must always tag up when fly balls are hit. He must have his foot on the bag, ready to push off and break hard for the plate. The situation is similar to that of a track star beginning a race with his feet in the blocks. On long, deep flies, the runner should wait until he sees the ball either disappear in the fielder's glove or drop to the ground. Although he could then walk home, he should still hustle hard. When medium outfield flies are hit the runner should listen to the base coach and know his own speed capabilities at the same time. If the runner doesn't go home, he should always bluff by running down three long steps. This will hurry up the relay home and possibly cause a bad throw to the catcher. Then he can come home. On short flies in the outfield or pop-ups to the infield, the runner should tag up and stay on third base.

Pickoffs are rarely tried at third base because an error on the throw could easily result in a run. But when the defensive team is behind or has a pitcher known for trying picks at any base, any time, the runner should be alert. Much more threatening to the runner are catcher pickoffs, especially if the runner runs third base as described earlier. He should not lean toward home at the end of his lead on each pitch and should take only the lead that he knows he can handle.

On passed balls and wild pitches, the runner must be ready to break instantly and slide hard, without hesitation. He must be the judge. If he feels the ball hasn't rolled far enough behind the catcher, he may bluff down and sprint back to third. If he decides to go, he must be very quick, for the pitcher will race in to cover the plate for a tag play. The runner must slide away from the pitcher to the right corner of the plate.

On bunted balls, the runner must be ready at any time for the squeeze if there are fewer than two outs. He must be sure to go the maximum distance down the third-base line. If the bunt is slow, out away from the plate, he should run hard. On a suicide bunt, he should just keep going! *He should never break, then hesitate, then break again.* He must go hard all the way and slide away from the catcher. But if the bunt is in the air, he should dive back very fast. On a safe-squeeze bunt, he waits until he sees the ball go slowly between fielders and then breaks hard. If the bunt is missed, he heads back fast, except on a suicide-squeeze bunt. In that case, he just keeps going, picks up speed, and takes the catcher out if he has the plate blocked well. By being tough, runners might score if the ball is dropped on the missed suicide-squeeze bunt play. But runners must be sure to touch the plate after the ball is dropped.

When runners are on first and third, the third-base runner must stay very alert. The first thing he must watch for is the sign from the coach. The runner needs to review in his mind the special timing for this tricky play. If he has forgotten or is confused about the timing, he should call time out. The runner should never go into a first-base–third-base running play without this understanding clear in his mind. Also, the runner should recall that there are seven different first-and-third running plays in baseball. Is the runner sure that he knows how to run each one? Remember, the only times a team doesn't score on this play are when the catcher's throw is cut off by pitcher, shortstop, or second baseman, or when the catcher fakes to second base, then fires to third. In all of these cases, the runner must dive back fast! He must make certain the catcher's throw to second base goes beyond a cutoff man.

How to Coach Third Base

The third-base coach never stays as busy as the coach on first, and his instructions are rather different from those of the first-base coach. He should do the following:

- Ask the runner to quickly recall the score, inning, and number of outs.

- Remind him how to run the third-base line on every pitch.
- Tell him to tag up on a long fly and run home. On a medium-depth fly, he may possibly run, but on a short fly, he will stay on third base.
- Tell the runner to go home on a slow grounder, but to stay at third on a hard grounder.
- Tell him to run on a grounder if the bases are loaded.
- If the bases are loaded and the count is full, tell the runner to go on the pitch.
- Remind the runner to watch for passed balls, wild pitches, and catcher pickoff attempts.
- Assist the runner with any trick plays, calling for a time-out if the runner doesn't understand.
- Assist the runner with the sign on a suicide-squeeze play, telling him to go after the pitcher has committed to the plate.
- Remind him of good outfielders' arms.
- Tell the runner if a hit goes through before he runs home.
- Be sure to tell the runner to tag up, and yell "Now" when the runner should take off after a caught fly ball.
- Be sure the runner goes down the line toward home in foul territory and retreats back to third base in fair territory.

How to Take Out a Catcher Who Blocks the Plate

Here is a skill that should be learned both to score a run and to keep the runner off the injury list. As he comes home hard and finds the catcher in the baseline about to receive the ball, the runner may move him by sliding or "rolling" home. The catcher either moves in front of the baseline, or he becomes fair game. The runner should not go around him or the catcher may have time to make the tag as the runner deviates in an arc. If the runner comes home and finds the catcher with the ball, the runner should not try to move the catcher out unless the runner is much heavier than the catcher. Weight and body build count here. The catcher has the advantage of padding and all kinds of protection. The catcher also usually has the advantage of weight, size, and muscle. But the catcher is also well set in his tracks and not moving, so the runner has the force of momentum as an advantage. The runner should not, however, try to move the

catcher if he has blocked the plate because then the runner will not be able to touch the plate. Nor should he try to go around the catcher bodily or in a reach; then the catcher will tag the runner before he reaches the plate.

Perhaps the only alternative in this case is for the runner to go over the catcher. In doing this, he aims high—for the catcher's chest and shoulders. The latter will move like a lever, pivoting backward as the runner hits his arms, hand, and glove. As the catcher barrels over on his back, the ball can easily be jarred from his grasp. If he drops the ball, the runner will be called safe. As the runner passes over him, he should look for the plate and touch it coming down, hoping the catcher drops the ball. If the catcher manages to hold the ball, the runner will probably be called out.

Assisting Runners Scoring at Home Plate

This is a very simple procedure. Here's how it's done. After a runner scores, he picks himself up quickly and moves 10 to 12 feet up the third-base foul line. As his teammate comes in, nearing 30 to 40 feet from home plate, the first player raises his hands in the air. If the second player should stand up, rather than slide home, he keeps his hands raised. If a slide is necessary, he drops both hands, pointing fingers toward the ground.

More Baserunning Tips

You have toured the bases and have encountered almost every situation possible at each base. This next section includes several specific baserunning hints.

An Important Defensive Maneuver: The Intentional Walk

Base runners should watch for this defensive play. The purpose of this play is to intentionally fill a base, thus producing a force play or a double play. This tactic at least ensures that runners do not advance or score and that a dangerous hitter does not get a chance to do damage with his bat. Usually base runners are placed so that first or second base is unoccupied. Some psychological damage can result, for the offensive team sees its big hitter given slight chance, and so they may hit into a situation where an out is possible at any base.

The success rate on this play is 100 percent, unless the pitcher becomes careless and brings the pitch in so close to the plate that the batter can reach it and swing at it.

The batter should watch carefully to see if the pitcher is getting the ball too close to the plate. The batter should call time out and ask the coach if he can hit the next pitch, if it is close. He then steps close to the plate in order to reach the pitch and tries for a base hit off the outside pitch.

If a runner on base sees that the pitches are too slow, he can surprise the catcher by stealing the next base. All runners must be alert for a ball dropped by the catcher or a wild pitch.

How to Run Bases on a Fly Ball Near the Foul Line

When running from first, second, or third base on a fly ball that looks like it might be fair or foul, no matter how deep the fly is, several things must be remembered. If the fly is caught, the runner must go back to the base and touch it before he can advance. If the fly is caught and he has tagged up properly, the runner may advance at his own peril. If a fielder must make the catch running away from the diamond on either foul line, any runner may be able to advance to the next base. The fielder must first catch the ball. Second, he must look to see where the runners are. Third, he has to recover his balance to make the throw, a long one that must be fast and accurate. The likelihood the fielder can do all this in time is slim. If a runner has any speed at all, he will beat the throw, but it will almost always be a fairly close play. The runner must slide hard.

How to Run When Trapped Between Bases

Running correctly between two bases when trapped in a rundown is a skill every base runner must know. Runners must never allow an easy tag, never quit hustling. They must never run into a ball intentionally, but make the defense throw many times before they can make the out. If the defense must lob back and forth more than three times, they lose some of their advantage. With every additional throw, they risk an error.

Always make the defense chase a runner to the next bag toward home. If the defense makes an error, you have gained the base you wanted. Bluff one way and go the other. If the runner takes two steps toward a base and then reverses his direction to the other base, he may get defense into the wrong throwing pattern. Thus, he may outrun the ball. When chased to a bag covered by a baseman, the runner drops low and hooks wide.

It is vital to remember if you get caught in a rundown to make sure your out takes enough time to allow the other runners to reach base safely. When a runner sees the ball waiting for him in a baseman's glove, and he knows he will be out, he should slide in such a way that the front foot kicks the ball out of the glove. He avoids spiking the fielder, but uses his foot to swipe at the glove and jar the ball loose. On applying the tag to the runner, the baseman may not have squeezed the ball tightly in his glove before the tag.

The Hidden-Ball Trick

The hidden-ball trick is as old as the hills. In years past, it was a favorite trick to get a ball club out of a jam and cut an offensive rally short. Some Little Leagues, and on up to the high-school-level leagues, forbid its use. Following are some runners' precautions regarding the hidden-ball trick.

As soon as a batter is safely on base, the first thing he should do is locate the ball. He must not step off any base until he actually sees the white of the baseball. The runner must not guess that the pitcher has it in his glove unless the pitcher's foot is on the rubber. Only then do you know the pitcher has the ball and that it is okay to lead off. Sometimes the ball is hidden inside a baseman's glove. If the runner doesn't see the ball, he should ask the first-base coach, "Who has the ball?" If the coach doesn't know, the runner should call time out and ask the umpire who has the ball. Do not call time in until both the umpire and runner see it. By this time, the defensive man who is holding the ball will reveal it and throw it back to the pitcher on the mound. He can be at the base of the mound or almost on the rubber, or he can toe the rubber; but he must not go into a pitching motion without the ball.

A team will usually try the hidden-ball trick just as a rally is getting started. The offensive team is having so much fun hitting that runners begin to let their guard down. Don't be careless. The defensive team may also try this when behind and desperate in the late innings. Of course, this trick may be pulled on runners at any time in any game. Watch for it at all times when two or more defensive men have huddled out on the diamond.

The umpire's responsibility on the hidden-ball trick is to know the rules of that league or level of baseball. Is it allowed in that league?

For more detail on the pitcher's balk rules, see chapter 3, "Section 8.05: The Pitcher's Balk."

How to Run Bases on Catcher's Pop-Up to the Deep Screen

This is the play that Pee Wee Reese tried in a World Series game in the 1950s. Reese was on first base, running for the Brooklyn Dodgers, and Yogi Berra was catcher for the New York Yankees. The Brooklyn batter lifted a high foul pop-up deep behind the plate. Yogi ripped off his mask and turned his back to the home plate and the diamond. He caught the fly ball inches from the screen in front of the press box. That was the first out. The screen was 120 feet from home plate, making a throw of 248 feet to second base. Yogi turned and fired a perfect strike to the shortstop covering second. Reese had decided to try for second base after the pop-up was caught. He was fast, and the race was almost a tie. But Yogi's throw got there a split second before Pee Wee arrived. That was the second out for a beautiful double play.

The moral of the story is simple. Don't try this trick when running from first or second base unless the runner is very fast, has tagged up, the screen is major-league distance from the plate (120 feet), and the catcher has a rather poor arm. Don't try it from second base, because the catcher has a shorter throw to third base, unless the runner is very fast. Never try it from third base to home, unless the pitcher forgets to cover home plate.

The Catcher's Role

When a runner takes too much lead and dares you to throw the ball, never throw to the base the runner is leaving. If he is off more than 25 feet toward the next base, he can easily run ahead and slide in safely while he is beating the two successive throws.

Instead of throwing, tell the pitcher to come in to cover home plate, then run out on the diamond with the ball held high near your ear and be ready to throw. Run toward the last base where the base runner *was*. Be sure to keep your eye on all other base runners in case one decides to break for the next base. Head the runner toward the other runners until two runners are on the same base. Then go over and tag them both with the ball. If another runner breaks from his bag, fire the ball to the base he is trying to steal.

Another option is for the catcher to walk a few steps out on the diamond and make a quick toss to the first baseman, so he can chase the runners into each other. The catcher should quickly go back to the plate and guard it in case a runner breaks for home. I prefer this second method because I do not want a pitcher injured while covering home on close plays. Of course, on this maneuver, the pitcher does cover home while the catcher is out tossing the ball to the first baseman.

When a third-base runner takes too much lead and dares you, never throw the ball to third base immediately. Move out toward third base and fire only when you see the runner dive back. You will nail him easily. If a catcher throws to third with a man 30 feet or more off the base, a very fast runner can break for home and slide, beating the two successive throws to the plate. A runner would always rather try to beat two throws instead of one.

Whenever the bases are loaded, the catcher should (a) never attempt a pickoff at first base, and (b) seldom try a pickoff at second base. If the bases are loaded and a runner takes too much lead off first base, let the pitcher pick him off. If the second-base runner is too far off base, fire a throw to second base only if the third-base runner presents little threat and has no lead. If there are two outs, a pickoff could end the inning and a big rally. But if you commit an error on a bases-loaded pickoff attempt, one run, and possibly two runs, will score.

Master Those Slides

Knowing how to slide is not only important to prevent injury, but it could mean a winning run. It's the ninth inning. The score is tied and a runner is on third, with two away. The batter connects and the runner races for home. A good slide could mean the difference between a third out or the winning run. Can the runner make it?

Smart players practice baserunning and sliding. They know when to streak for second, the right time to steal third. In a close play, they avoid the tag by sliding safely into the side away from the fielder. Smart runners watch the coaches at first and third. If the coach has his palms down, parallel to the ground, he is signaling to slide. When learning to slide, runners should go all out and learn to do it well. The coach must be sure they are willing to practice and know what to do. All players should master the straight-in, hook, and headfirst slides.

The Straight-In or Stand-Up Slide

This type of slide is used to come hard up to a base, slide in, let the momentum knock the ball out of the baseman's glove, get up off the sliding leg on the front outstretched leg, and continue forward fast. It is a good slide when the runner is forced, but not a good slide on a tag play where the baseman is trying to reach a part of the runner's body. Practice this slide both to the right and left sides of the bag.

The straight-in slide is fairly simple. A runner moves directly toward the base and starts the slide with his left or right foot. Lowering the body, he bends his forward leg, curling it to the rear. The other leg is extended toward the base with the foot kept parallel to the ground. The slide is made feet-first with the arms outstretched. Overcome any fears runners may have by practicing the slide over and over. The movement soon becomes natural. The goal is to relax and make a full slide at each practice. For the straight-in slide, be sure to point the feet toward the base, curl the lead foot behind the hips, and stretch the opposite leg toward the base.

The Hook Slide

This is a beautiful maneuver. As the runner reaches the point of takeoff on his slide, he merely tucks one leg under the body, points the other out very wide, and drops all of his body to the ground. The runner's entire back should touch the ground as he slides away from a tag. The back foot should hook the edge of the bag and maintain contact with it. Use this slide on close plays at a base where a tag must be applied. Practice this type of slide to both

sides of the bag. The hook slide offers a big advantage: it helps the runner present a smaller target.

In making the hook, a player slides into the side of the base that is least defended. He begins the motion with either foot. The weight is brought back toward the ground. When sliding to the right, the weight is behind his right leg. The runner then hooks a corner of the base with the toe of his left foot. His legs are spread and extended. Remember these points: Direct the body to the right or left of the base; when sliding to the right, support the weight on the upper right leg; extend both legs and hook a corner of the bag with the toe of the left foot.

The Headfirst or Belly Slide

Pepper Martin in the 1930s and Pete Rose in the 1960s perfected this slide. The runner takes off at a proper distance from the base, puts both hands out in front of the body, and slides on his stomach and chest. He touches the base with either hand and keeps it on the bag. This slide takes more momentum because so much of the body is in contact with the ground for a long time. There is considerable risk to the head, face, and neck area on this slide. Also, the risk of injuring the hands, arms, chest, and belly is great. There are no sliding pads covering a runner's chest and stomach.

Remember, on sliding plays, either the baseman or the thrown ball can also injure a runner. Some basemen apply the tag very hard. However, some fast runners prefer this slide and are willing to risk injury. They say it is faster and easier to do.

Six Methods of Getting the First Run of a Game

It is very important to get the first run of a ball game. First, it gives the pitcher a lead to carry out on the mound. He can pitch very differently with a lead of one or more runs. Second, it gives your team the momentum, the good start, that feeling of "we're going to win this ball game." Third, the other team now has to score two runs to beat you. This causes them to play a different kind of game, possibly taking away some of their running and bunting early in the game. In high school and lower levels of ball, only seven-inning games are played. Getting the first run in a short game puts early pressure on opponents.

When your team is ahead, it can play a more wide-open style of baseball. It can either "work for the insurance run," or "get one per inning," or play for the "big inning." It would be interesting to see what we would find if scorebooks of every baseball game were examined. I would bet that the team that scores the first run wins more, or even most games. Let's work for that first run, using one of the following six patterns of play. A team must practice each of these methods if it expects to open the first inning of a game with confidence for success.

Method 1

First man gets on. Bunt him from first to third base on one good sacrifice bunt, then score him from third base after one out.

Take the team's fastest man and use him as the lead-off batter. Tell him to get on base either by earning a walk or by hitting away, whichever seems appropriate. When the batter arrives at first base, give him the steal sign, the special sign indicating he should go on to third base on the bunt. You are now bunting and stealing on the same pitch.

Signal the batter to bunt down the third-base line. He must hit a slow bunt, so the third baseman has to field it. The third baseman fields the bunt, fires a long throw to first base and is now too far in to go back to cover third. Someone forgets to cover third base! The runner from first rounds second base and keeps going to third, sliding hard into the bag. The first baseman will fire a long throw back to third-base area. Even if someone covers, it will be too late. Or he may throw it into left field, scoring a run the easy way. If the runner stays on third, he is there with only one out. There are many ways to score him from third with only one away. You may wish to squeeze-bunt the third-base runner home with the next batter.

Method 2

First runner gets on. Sacrifice-bunt him to second base, then bunt him home on a double-suicide squeeze, scoring him while the second out is made.

The leadoff man drag bunts and beats it out. The next batter sacrifices him to second base, making the first out. The third batter lays down a perfect slow bunt in front of the third baseman, who throws to first. On the bunt, the second-base runner steals, rounds third, keeps coming home, and beats the relay home from first base to the catcher. The bunter is out at first base. The first run scores and there are now two outs.

Method 3

First man gets on. Fake-bunt him to second base, then sacrifice-bunt him from second base to third base. Score him from third base on a suicide squeeze, safety squeeze, or sacrifice fly. Score one run, making two outs.

The first batter gets on first in any fashion. The second batter fake-bunts at the ball and the first-base runner steals on the fake. Now bunt him to third on the next pitch. The batter is out at first base. Now suicide-squeeze the third-base runner home, or wait for a sacrifice fly or a base hit. The runner scores, but there are two outs.

Method 4

First man bunts to get on. The next batter pulls a hit-and-run play to right field. With runners now on first and third base, work an early double steal and score the first run with either none or one out.

The first man up bunts to get on, and the second batter looks for an outside pitch. He hits softly over second base into right field. The first-base runner goes and lands safely on third, and the batter makes it to first base. The coach now calls for the early type of first-and-third-base double steal. Pitcher may balk in a run at this point, or he may throw the ball into center field if the baseman doesn't cover second base. Or, the third-base runner scores, beating the two throws. On this pattern of plays, you could score the first run of the game, with no outs, and a man on either second or third. You can inflict much damage by this method.

Method 5

Bunt the first man on. A hit-and-run play to right field puts runners on second and third base. Run a double suicide-squeeze bunt and score two runs with only one out.

The first man gets on with a drag bunt down the line. The second man drills a hit-and-run single between first base and second base on an outside pitch. The first-base runner, who stole on the pitch, arrives at third base, and the batter who hit to right field makes it to second base because the throw from right field arrives at third too late. The coach now calls for the double-suicide squeeze. Both men should score on a good bunt, if it is a slow dribbler in front of third base. The batter is thrown out at first base, but two runs score with only one out lost.

Method 6

Bunt to get on. Move the man from first to third base on a sacrifice bunt. Use a sacrifice fly or base hit to score the first run with one or two outs.

The first man up gets on first base any way he can. The next batter bunts the man from first to third base with a two-base sacrifice. The bunter is thrown out at first base, and now a man is on third with one out. The third-base runner can score now with a hit, a sacrifice fly, an error, or by any other means.

Chapter

5

Stealing Mechanics

In the early days of baseball, stealing was not foremost in the minds of players. The emphasis was on hitting the ball and not taking chances. But approaching the turn of the century, more and more teams realized that stealing a base was not so difficult. By 1900 they began to study every aspect of the pitcher, the catcher, and the infielders, with the purpose of refining the runner's game. Ty Cobb not only studied the requirements of stealing first, second, third, and home, but added another vital ingredient: intimidation of the defense. Cobb's aggressive approach initiated general interest in running the bases. He challenged defenses and set a precedent for the other great runners in baseball history. Pepper Martin, Jackie Robinson, Maury Wills, Rod Carew, Lou Brock, Tim Raines, Rickey Henderson, and others really put running pressure on the opposition. And the crowds loved it!

In this section, I will give a breakdown of the factors that can help runners steal bases. Here are the main factors that affect the art of base stealing:

1. The pitcher's characteristics
2. The catcher's characteristics
3. Game situation: the count, number of outs, and score
4. The particular base attempted

Portions of the material on pp. 107-114 were adapted from *Sports Illustrated BASEBALL*, © 1983 Time Inc., by Jerry Kindall. Used with permission.

The Pitcher's Characteristics

If the pitcher throws a very fast ball on most pitches, then a runner's stealing time is reduced. Stealing off a fastball pitcher is difficult if his other pitching mechanics are also sound. If the pitcher throws a lot of "junk," such as breaking or off-speed pitches and knuckleballs, then the runner has more time to steal. The catcher has longer to wait for the ball, and there will be more balls passed and dropped by the catcher on breaking pitches. It is, of course, a gamble; try to figure out when the breaking pitches are coming up. The pitcher who has a good move to a base is a definite threat. He will worry the runner more, preventing him from moving off base far enough to assure a steal. Watch the pitcher's leg kick. A high kick will slow his delivery, and runners can steal more often. A high leg kick is a good indicator of speed, leverage, and whip; however, it gives runners time to steal a base.

A pitcher who does not look over to a base often is an easy steal. He simply doesn't see the runner inching out, taking more and more lead. Eventually he will make the fatal mistake of pitching to the plate after allowing the runner too much lead. On the other hand, many pitchers throw over to a base too often. This keeps runners closer to the bag, but it can also work against the pitcher by breaking his rhythm and concentration. When such a pitcher is on the mound, the runner will need to study the pitcher in order to go during delivery of the pitch. If a pitcher delivers quickly from the stretch, then stealing will be more difficult. The pitcher gets rid of the ball very quickly, with no wasted time or motion. Study this trait.

Some pitchers and catchers collaborate and throw pitchouts during stealing situations. The runner must study the catcher's pattern and outguess the batter so as not to steal on a pitchout. Watch the head and shoulders of the pitcher on a pickoff throw. Study the upper part of his body. See if the pitcher exhibits unusual movements of these parts only when he throws to a base. Most pitchers will, inadvertently, telegraph their intentions. Look for patterns to key on. It is the head and shoulder moves that cause a balk. Coaches may appeal to an umpire any time the pitcher balks. Remind umpires to watch the pitcher's head and upper body. Finally, watch the front of the pitcher's knee and lower leg, especially if he is a left-hander. Knee characteristics of southpaws on pickoff attempts at first base are very deceptive. A left-handed pitcher may raise his leg, but in midair he will set it down toward first base. Runners must be careful they are not caught too far off base or leaning toward second base. It is extremely difficult to steal second base in this situation. More detail on stealing off the pitcher is presented later in this chapter.

The Catcher's Characteristics

Most characteristics of a catcher can be picked up either from watching pregame warm-ups or from good scouting reports. Of prime concern is the catcher's arm. Watch for a real "shotgun arm." Of course, if the defense has a slow-delivering pitcher, a runner can still steal off the strong-armed catcher. The catcher is rather helpless to throw out the runner after a very slow delivery. Time of release is as important to a catcher as strength of arm. If the catcher gets the ball out of his glove instantly, it will be tough to steal from him, even with a slower pitcher on the mound. Release time is critical to stealing a base.

Some catchers throw strongly from a fastball pitch, but their accuracy is very uneven. Such a catcher is easy to steal on if a runner can get the jump on the pitcher. Watch for this in the catcher's warm-ups during infield practice. Perhaps the catcher throws a rising or tailing ball that pulls a baseman off the bag so the runner cannot be tagged quickly.

Some teams use a lot of catcher pickoffs at any base. Usually, the catcher loves to show off his arm. After an inning or so, a runner can pick up the pattern and simply take his normal lead off base on each pitch, but hustle or even dive back if such a catcher is behind the plate. There is never any excuse for a runner to be picked off by a catcher at any base.

It shouldn't take an offense long to see which pitch a catcher calls for, with a particular pitcher, with two strikes on the batter. If the catcher always calls for a down-breaking curve or an off-speed breaking pitch with two strikes, this may be the time to steal. The ball is delivered more slowly and may be in the dirt, or it may be outside and hard to handle. The pitcher throws this pitch to strike out the batter, not to hold down the runner. Similarly, if runners know the opposing catcher has trouble digging bad pitches out of the dirt, then stealing is easier on those pitches. If a coach knows the catcher does not stay in front of bad pitches, blocking them with his body and the outside knee, he knows it is then easier to steal. Finally, coaches should know whether the opposing catcher calls for many pitchouts. Study the catcher to know when the pitchouts are used by the batter. A runner should not get caught trying a steal on a pitchout.

Game Situation: Count, Number of Outs, and Score

Smart base runners are into the game at all times. They know the score, outs, and count, and the characteristics of the pitcher and catcher. Experience tells them when and when not to steal. Because runners must be fully alert to outguess the defensive team on a certain pitch, the bases are no place for a "baseball dreamer," a player who is asleep.

Which Base You Are Attempting to Steal

How and when the runner steals depends on which base he is attempting. The amount of lead pitchers allow is different at each bag. The score, number of outs, and count on the batter all determine whether the runner can successfully steal a particular base at that time. Some runners feel that stealing third base is easier than stealing second. Stealing home, of course, is the most difficult. No one who is not extremely fast on the base paths should ever try it. Even so, it is a rare play and seldom attempted.

Making the Turn at First Base

As soon as a runner determines that the ball is through the infield, he must run between the chalk lines to within 30 feet of first base. Then he swings to his right, creating a wide arc 12 feet into foul territory, crossing the bag going full speed toward second base. The 12-foot arc is enough to give the body control without affecting speed or causing the runner to stumble as he makes the turn. More important, it puts the runner in a straight path from first to second base. Anything less than a 12-foot arc will carry the runner out toward right field as he makes the turn, and anything more is wasted time and effort. Ideally, the runner should hit first base with the right foot so that the next stride with the left foot is straight toward second base. If this can't be done, he should not risk stumbling and losing time trying to stagger the steps. He should then go for the front inside corner of the bag with either foot.

As an aggressive, alert runner, a player can force errors in the outfield by running full speed as he makes the turn at first base, continuing toward second until the outfielder fields the ball cleanly and throws to second base. On a single to left field, for example, a runner can go nearly halfway to second base before braking to a stop and retreating to first base. On a single to center field, a runner could worry the outfielder into a fumble or bad throw by going one third of the way toward second. Of course, a runner must use more caution on a ball hit to right field. A quick throw from the right fielder to the first baseman could pick him off if the turn is too long. In any case, he should run full speed on a ball hit to the outfield, make the 12-foot arc across first base, and challenge the outfielder.

Figure 5.1 Making the turn at first base.

When the runner returns to first base, the retreat is made with eyes on the ball and the chest facing the throw from the outfield. A bad throw to second base could allow the first-base runner to advance.

The Elements of Stealing Second Base

Safe on first, the runner is now in a position on the diamond where every ball player is expected to steal occasionally. Most runners will try to steal second base, even those of less than average speed. Since more runners make it to first than any other base, steal attempts on second base will occur most often. Players must, therefore, learn this one well. They should remember that the catcher must throw a greater distance to second base than to any other, exactly 127.26 feet from the plate. If the runner has a 15-foot lead, he has to run only 75 feet. The race is almost always a tie.

Most base runners use the crossover step as their first move toward second base in the steal attempt. The upper body is thrown vigorously toward second base. Reaching out with the left arm, the runner pivots on the ball of the right foot while pushing off hard with the left foot toward second base. Several things are important in this first explosive move:

- Stay low during the first stride.
- Step first with the left foot directly toward second base, not toward the mound or shortstop.
- The arms should instantly begin powering the body in coordination with the legs.

Make the first several strides toward second base short, driving, choppy ones until full speed is reached. After two or three strides, look at the plate to see what is happening to the pitch. The general rule is to take two steps and look. Turning the head slightly will tell the runner whether he should (a) continue, (b) stop (on a pop fly), (c) break up a double play (on a ground ball), (d) go on to third base (on a base hit), or (e) round second base on a passed ball or wild pitch. Unfortunately many runners are tricked into double plays or held between bases because they do not know where the ball is, particularly since turning the head after the second

stride and reading the ball off the bat is such a simple matter.

There will be times when the runner breaks prematurely for second base as the pitcher tries to pick him off at first. The best option in this event is to go full speed toward second base and try to beat the first baseman's throw or arrive safely on a bad throw. Such situations generally occur with a left-handed pitcher who has a deceptive move to first base.

On a hit-and-run, the runner's role at first base is very simple: He must absolutely avoid a pick-off. He must be certain the pitcher has delivered to the plate before he breaks for second base; after two steps, he should look toward the plate. Obviously, the coach has decided the runner will more likely advance on the hit-and-run than on the straight steal, so the runner must not ruin the strategy through carelessness.

Types of Steals

There are four types of steals of second base:

1. Straight steal on the pitcher's delivery
2. Delayed steal on the pitcher's throw to first
3. Delayed steal on the catcher's throw to first
4. Delayed steal on the catcher's throw back to the pitcher

Straight Steal. This is the most common one. Runner simply takes the maximum lead, proven to be no more than 14 feet for the player of average speed. As the pitcher commits himself to the plate, the runner breaks, runs to second base with full acceleration, and slides hard with a hook, away from the inside of the diamond.

Delayed Steal on the Pitcher's Throw to First. A delayed steal is defined as any steal attempted after the pitch has reached the catcher. If there is a slight delay by the runner after the catcher receives the ball, then the play is one of several types of delayed steals. Generally, delayed steals can be attempted in three ways. First, the runner goes to the next base as the catcher throws to the base where the runner began the play. Second, the runner goes to the next base as the pitcher attempts a pickoff throw to the original base. Third, the runner goes to the next base as the catcher throws the ball back to the pitcher. These can be attempted at any of the

Figure 5.2 The steal from first to second base: The first several strides should be short, choppy ones until full speed is reached.

three bases, but only an incredibly fast runner could successfully work them at all bases. Very few runners have ever done this.

When a runner is too far off base and a pitcher decides to try a pickoff, it is possible to steal second base by breaking, from at least 14 feet off first, as the pitcher releases the ball. The runner must be quite fast to make this work, and he must slide hard. The throw from the pitcher to the first baseman, the catch and throw to second base, and the tag must all be perfect. If any one of these things goes awry, the runner will win the race. Coaches should never try this play with slow runners.

To execute a delayed steal off first base, take a large lead, about 20 feet. The runner should act as though he is going to steal, but steps too far off first base to come back safely, leaning back just slightly toward first. As he sees the catcher's arm rise and the ball leave his fingertips, the runner should shift his weight and head to second base. A quick, fast initial step is vital, as well as a hard slide. The ball will go from the catcher to first base to the shortstop covering second base. It travels 180 feet, while base runner runs 70 feet. The fast runner has a 50-50 chance on this play. The defense must be very quick and do everything perfectly.

In a second delayed-steal option, the runner takes a normal lead off first base, about 15 feet. The runner pretends he is coming back to the bag and leans slightly in that direction. As the catcher lobs the ball back to the pitcher on the mound, the runner shifts his weight back toward second base, getting the fast initial step. He goes into second base, sliding hard. The runner is beating the lob throw of 61 feet, plus another throw of 66 feet to the second-base area, while he travels 75 feet. The time advantage is with the defensive team. However, the element of surprise is in the runner's favor, and no one may be covering second base to field the pitcher's throw. The runner may end up on third base after the error. This play is particularly effective against catchers who hesitate or throw slowly to the pitcher.

Delayed Steal on the Catcher's Throw to First. This steal is executed on the catcher's throw to first base after the pitch. The catcher's pickoff throw will leave his fingers as the runner leads 14 feet off first base. As the runner sees the ball leave the catcher's hand, he should take off for second base. Again, if the ball is mishandled by the catcher, first

baseman, or the infielder covering second base on the throw, then the runner will win.

Delayed Steal on the Catcher's Throw Back to Pitcher. This is the third type of delayed-steal play. It works beautifully, for in it is the extreme element of surprise. Again, remember, coaches must not run any of these three delayed-steal options unless the runner is exceptionally fast and has natural quickness and "first step burst."

On this play, the runner again takes his maximum lead of 14 feet, and the instant the catcher releases the ball to the pitcher, he breaks for second base. The pitcher catches the ball and everyone yells, "There he goes." Remember, the pitcher's back is toward the runner. The pitcher will whirl and throw to an infielder covering second base. The runner will win the race if the catcher, pitcher, or second baseman bobbles the ball. Also, the runner wins if second base is not quickly covered on the steal, or if the pitcher's throw is not on target.

How to Steal Second Base Off the Pitcher

Good base runners at all levels of the game learn to study the peculiarities of each pitcher they face. No two pitchers will be exactly alike. The runner must first find out how much lead each pitcher will allow before he throws over to first base on a pickoff attempt. Most teams find that 10 feet is the maximum. Remember, the runner does not steal on the catcher. He always steals on the pitcher.

Left-Handed Pitchers. Be sure the runner steps in a direct line toward second base. Watch the pitcher's right shoulder carefully. He will usually move that part of his body first. The shoulder has to come around toward the runner before the pitcher can make the pickoff throw. Very few lefties can get much of a pickoff throw to first base and keep both shoulders in line with home plate. Excellent pickoff moves by lefties usually fool the runner with the leg kick. Watch the lower leg and foot. At the highest point of the pitcher's leg kick, the runner will see the leg move very slightly toward him. Don't watch the knee only, but the knee, lower leg, and foot. If the runner sees either the right shoulder move or the leg and knee kick toward him, he should get back fast.

Of course, when running from first base, the runner learns that he cannot take as much lead off first on a leftie as he can on a rightie. Lefties are open to the runner. They can see the runner at all parts of their stretch and delivery.

Right-Handed Pitchers. The same guidelines given in the preceding section apply, with the following exceptions:

Runners can take longer leads (no more than 14 feet) and get a better jump on the right-hander, because the pitcher's back is turned to him. Right-handed pitchers usually throw to first base less often than a left-hander will. Again step directly toward second base and watch the pitcher's left shoulder carefully. The pitcher must usually move that part of the body first in order to deliver the pickoff throw.

Remember that righties pick off with sheer quickness those runners who take too big a lead, but lefties do it with a deceptive move. Don't get caught leaning on any type of pitcher. Keep your body weight on your feet and toes so you can break either left or right with equal speed. Remember, too, that when a right-hander lifts his leg, he is delivering to the plate. Otherwise, he would have to balk. Runners who steal off right-handers do so by taking advantage of a weakness in the pitcher's delivery. If they want to improve their stealing, runners must learn to study the pitcher very carefully. (For a description of the balk rule, see "Section 8.05: The Pitcher's Balk" in chapter 3.)

The Elements of Stealing Third Base

When a runner reaches second base, he must be careful to assure every opportunity of reaching home. A slow runner should not try for home. A base runner embarrasses himself and, worse, kills the rally if he allows himself to get picked off at second base.

With fewer than two outs, a runner should take the lead off second base in a straight line toward third. The primary lead can normally be up to 20 feet without danger because the shortstop and second baseman won't hold the runner tight at this base. Watch the pitcher, and out of the corner of the left eye, watch the second baseman lest he break for a pickoff attempt. The third-base coach is

Figure 5.3 The long and explosive initial step of a steal attempt.

a

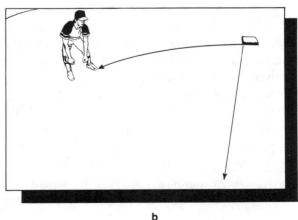

b

Figure 5.4 Types of leads off second base: with fewer than two outs (a), or with two outs (b).

responsible for urging the runner back to second base if the shortstop breaks behind him for a pick-off. If neither middle infielder decides to hold the runner on, the third-base coach can then talk the runner into a longer lead, perhaps up to 30 feet. The choreography would be the same as at first base: right foot lead; left foot shuffle; right foot lead; and left foot shuffle.

When the pitcher delivers to the plate, the runner should take a secondary lead by shuffling several times toward third base with his chest pointing toward home and eyes focused intently on the strike zone. As the pitch enters the strike zone, the runner should be completing the second shuffle, with his weight on the right foot. With fewer than two outs, he does not try to advance on a routine or hard-hit ground ball to the left side of the infield. The shortstop could field the grounder and make the throw to third, or the third baseman could field it and tag the runner before he reaches third base or catch him in a rundown. All of these are "sucker plays," and unwise baserunning of this kind can kill the inning.

When the ball is hit, read the direction of the batted ball. If a ground ball is hit at the runner or to the left of him, except to the pitcher, he advances to third base. If the ground ball is hit hard or routinely to his right, the runner holds and retreats to second base with his chest pointing toward the play. Of course, if the ground ball to the right gets through the infield, he advances to third base. If a ground ball to the right is a high chopper or slow roller, a runner can gauge that and advance safely.

The best time to steal third base is with one out and your team ahead, tied, or one run behind. Many great base stealers feel that taking third base is generally easier than stealing second because the pitcher, middle infielders, and third baseman are more concerned with the batter than the runner, thus permitting him a much longer lead. Still, the runner must have a good lead and a good jump. Having only one of the two is not enough. By increasing the primary lead of 18 to 20 feet to 25 to 28 feet and by keeping the body moving toward third base as the pitcher commits the delivery to the plate, the runner guarantees a quicker jump and a shorter run for the steal.

As the great base runners will admit, stealing third base is no easy job. The distance of the catcher's throw to third base is 90 feet, compared to 128 feet to second base. However, this is equalized by the runner in two ways. The third-base steal is so rare that the running team always has the element of surprise in its favor. The pitcher and catcher will allow runners longer leads off second base than they do off first base. Catchers try fewer pickoff throws at second, too.

To steal third base, the runner must, first of all, be very fast. Only the fastest two or three players on a team should attempt this steal. Second, a runner must watch the pitcher, shortstop, and second baseman, and lull them into believing he poses no threat to steal. Third, the best time to steal third is when the runner's team is ahead. If the runner is thrown out, it is not critical. If he makes it, the runner adds insult to injury. This steal is important because there are so many more ways to score from third base than there are from second base. So, it's often worth the gamble, especially in the early innings when the team is attempting to build an insurmountable lead.

To execute this steal, the runner should

- take the maximum lead without fear of pitcher pickoff,
- use a fast initial step,
- slide hard into third base,
- use a low hook slide,
- slide to the outfield side of the bag, and
- get up immediately, in case of a wild throw or error.

Types of Steals

The four types of steals from second base described in the following paragraphs are these:

1. Straight steal of third base
2. Delayed steal on pitcher's throw to second
3. Delayed steal on catcher's throw to second
4. Delayed steal on catcher's throw back to pitcher

Straight Steal of Third Base. This is the most commonly executed steal. The runner simply takes the maximum lead, with momentum toward third. The catcher has a throw of only 90 feet to the third baseman, while the runner must run and slide perhaps 62 feet. It will always be a close race. This is a daring play. Coaches should never use this play unless the runner is very fast, with great acceleration on the first step.

Delayed Steal on the Pitcher's Throw to Second.
When a runner is too far off base and knows the pitcher will try to pick him off at second base, it is possible to steal third. The runner should break 25 to 28 feet off second and go to third as the pitcher releases the ball to second base. The runner must be very quick, and slide hard into third base. Always hook slide away to the right side of the bag, for the throw will come from the second baseman. The throw from the pitcher to the second baseman, his catch, and then his throw to the third baseman must all be perfect. If any one of these goes awry, or if there is hesitation between them, the runner will arrive safely.

Delayed Steal on the Catcher's Throw to Second. After the pitch, the catcher's attempted pickoff throw will leave his fingers as the runner leads 25 to 28 feet off second base. If the runner is 28 feet away, he will probably win the race to third base. As he sees the ball leave the catcher's hand, the runner takes off and slides hard into third.

Delayed Steal on the Catcher's Throw Back to Pitcher. On this type of play, the runner again takes the maximum lead. The instant he sees the catcher release the ball back to the pitcher, he breaks for third base, running 62 feet and sliding hard to the right side of the bag as the pitcher catches the ball, whirls, and fires to the third baseman. The runner will win the race if catcher, pitcher, or third baseman bobbles the ball or hesitates, or if either throw is not on the mark.

How to Execute the Fake Steal Off First, Second, or Third Base

The fake-steal sign is an important one. It may be as vital as the steal sign, for it also sets up the steal when the runner wants to execute it. Runners completely deceive the defensive team on every pitch.

The coach gives the runner or runners the fake-steal sign. Runners wait until they are sure the pitcher is delivering to the plate. On the pitch, they should run in the same style they would if actually stealing, not changing the footwork pattern in any way. They should go as far off base as seems safe, then hurry back as the catcher receives the ball. Of course, if runners start back any later, they will certainly be picked off. If a runner does this on every pitch, or every other pitch, or only on certain pitches, it will confuse the defense on every pitch.

The Elements of Stealing Home

On third base the runner stands only 90 feet from completing the long journey around the diamond. There are a number of ways for him to score now. His first concern at third is not to do anything foolhardy to negate the work it took to get him there. Never get picked off at third base!

Leading Off at Third Base

1. The primary lead should be only as far toward home plate as the third baseman is from the bag. If the third baseman is only 3 feet from third, that is the extent of your primary lead. If he is 12 feet off the bag when the pitcher comes to his set or begins his wind-up, the runner can be 12 feet down the line. This holds true up to 20 feet.

2. Always take the primary and secondary leads in foul territory. If a batted ball hits the runner while on the baseline or in fair territory, the runner is automatically out; if the runner is in foul territory when the batted ball strikes him, there is no penalty.

3. If the runner leads off the bag in foul territory, he should come back to the bag in fair territory. Once the pitch hits the catcher's mitt, the runner jams his right foot into the ground to stop the secondary lead; then he turns and retreats to third base in fair territory. By retreating in fair ground, the runner obscures the catcher's view toward the bag, and if the catcher throws to the third baseman in a pickoff attempt, the ball may hit the runner and allow him to score.

The Primary Lead. Once the runner establishes the primary lead in foul ground equidistant from the bag with the third baseman, his position should be essentially the same as when he took his lead at first base. He should be facing the pitcher, with his feet spread more than a shoulders' width apart, with his weight on the balls of his feet. From this position, the runner can get back to the bag if there is a pickoff attempt by the pitcher. Or he can begin his secondary lead once he is certain the pitcher is delivering.

a

b

c

Figure 5.5 Leads off third base and tagging up.

The Secondary Lead. When taking a secondary lead off third base, point the chest toward the mound, keep the eyes turned toward home plate, and step first toward the plate with the left foot, following it with a series of shuffle steps. As the runner begins the shuffles, it is important that he fix his eyes intently on the strike zone, where, of course, the ball will or will not be hit. Time the shuffles so that as the pitch enters the strike zone, most of the runner's weight is on the right foot; then he can react instantly to what may happen at the plate. Taking this type of aggressive yet controlled lead, the runner can also practice the "down angle" concept of scoring on a ground ball. This occurs with one out and the runner's team ahead, tied, or one run down; the runner can score on most ground balls, even with the infield playing in to cut that run off at the plate.

Here's how it works. Suppose the pitcher is delivering from the set position, and the third baseman allows the runner a 15-foot primary lead. The secondary lead will have carried the runner 25 to 28 feet down the line from third base, or slightly more than 60 feet from home plate when the grounder is hit. At that instant, if the weight is primarily on the right foot and he sees the ball go "down angle," the runner can break home immediately, using a crossover left stride, and beat most infielders' throws home. Of course, if the ground ball is hit to the pitcher or hit hard at an infielder playing shallow, the runner will likely be out. But most ground balls are hit to an infielder's right or left, and many are slow hits. This majority of ground balls will allow the base runner to score—provided he reads the "down angle" immediately.

From the proper secondary lead with fewer than two outs, if the runner reads "line drive" off the bat, he should freeze and hustle back to third base if the line drive is caught. If the runner reads "up angle" off the bat, meaning fly ball, he must immediately retreat to third base and tag up for the possible score after the catch.

Types of Steals

Again, there are four types of steals from third base in which runners are trying to score by stealing home:

1. Straight steal on the pitcher's delivery

2. Delayed steal on the pitcher's throw to third base

3. Delayed steal on the catcher's throw to third base

4. Delayed steal on the catcher's throw back to the pitcher

All of these are rare plays attempted either by very, very fast runners or by coaches who are desperate. Be that as it may, stealing home is also one of the sport world's most exciting maneuvers. Let's examine these four types of steals, and perhaps, in the minds of some runners, it will move at least into the realm of possibility.

a

b

Figure 5.6 The secondary lead off third and the run home.

The Straight Steal. This is the most difficult of the four steals to execute. The fast runner pits uncanny swiftness and daring against the blinding speed of the pitched baseball. In the history of professional baseball, perhaps only two dozen men have ever lived who could execute this play successfully. This does not mean that in the lower levels of the game the play would not likely be more successful.

To execute this play, the runner must, first, be gifted with nearly blinding speed. Second, he must execute it with the pitcher's windup. Do not ever try it during the pitcher's stretch. Third, the runner must hope the pitcher throws either a high-outside straight ball, a slow-breaking curve, a knuckleball, or any kind of pitch low and in the dirt. Fourth, he hopes the catcher bobbles the ball or that he drops the ball after he makes the tag. Finally, there is always hope that the umpire will make a bad call—in the runner's favor. If any one of these occurs, the runner will probably be safe at home plate.

Be sure the runner comes down the line the maximum distance before the pitcher delivers. On this play, the batter should stay in the batting stance, perhaps even fake a bunt. Then the batter must step back out of the way at the last moment so that the umpire does not call interference and nullify the run. Be sure the runner slides to the correct side of the plate, toward foul ground.

Delayed Steal on the Pitcher's Throw to Third Base. This is easier to execute than a straight steal of home. If the runner is too far off third base and the pitcher decides to pick him off while in the stretch, it is possible the runner can steal home by breaking, from 20 feet off third, as the pitcher releases the ball to the third baseman. If all catches and throws by the defense are less than perfect, or if one of the infielders hesitates, then the fast runner will probably make it safely to the plate.

Delayed Steal on the Catcher's Throw to Third Base. Also easier to execute than a straight steal of home, this play is executed on the catcher's throw to third base. For this reason, be sure the runner stays inside the foul line in fair territory. The runner comes way down the line, intentionally, and the catcher attempts the pickoff. As the runner, 28 feet down the line, sees the ball leave the catcher's fingers toward third base, he breaks hard on the first step, accelerates, and slides hard into the plate, hooking the right side. If the throw is bad, the ball is fumbled, or the defense hesitates, the run will score.

Delayed Steal on the Catcher's Throw Back to the Pitcher. On this play, the runner must take the maximum lead, and the instant the catcher receives the ball, he leans back toward third to make the catcher think he is retreating. The runner must keep his body weight balanced, ready to break for home. The instant the catcher releases the ball to the pitcher, the runner leans toward home, accelerating fast on that first step, and goes into the plate sliding hard. The pitcher throws the ball back home for the tag. Any defensive errors and the runner will probably be safe.

6

The Hit Ball: What Runners Should Do

In most of the 28 running plays presented in this text, the batter may take the pitch. But what should runners do when the ball is hit? This chapter presents charts and diagrams giving directions to runners for each of the 36 possible types of hit balls. According to the number of runners on base, the 36 kinds of hit balls can be grouped, as follows, into eight possible running situations:

- No one on, only the batter at the plate
- Man on first base only
- Man on second base only
- Man on third base only
- Men on first and second bases only
- Men on second and third bases only
- Men on first and third bases only
- Bases loaded

Use of the 36 Hit-Ball Charts

The charts that make up the body of this chapter show the type of hit at the top of the page and the eight possible combinations of runners in the left-hand column. Three columns to the right give directions for the runner at each base. As far as I know, these charts and the running directions they give are unique. They have been carefully checked by other coaches. These charts are one of the main objectives of this manual, and I created them with the following uses in mind:

- A coach could use them to review skills in practice, putting runners on bases and practicing one chart per day, going through every possible hit situation in a very short time.
- Coaches could use them as a convenient guide to check their runners after a play to see if they ran the bases correctly.
- Young coaches who need to study and analyze what runners should do could use the charts as a learning tool.

Before proceeding to the charts, let's review some general rules for grounders and flies.

Running on Hit Ground Balls

Man on first base. If the ball is hit to any part of the infield, runner must go at the crack of the bat; he is forced. Try to break up the double play.

Man on second base. If the ball is hit to the left side, retreat back toward second base to a lead of two big steps. Wait for the throw to first base. Runner should stay on second, unless he is very fast.

If he has great speed, go to third base on the throw to first base.

Go hard on any ball hit up the middle. The second baseman or shortstop moving in to take the grounder near second base will be unable to get the runner sliding into third base.

On a ball hit to the right side of the diamond, the runner should beat the long throw to third base. The defense will probably throw to first base, allowing him to advance to third.

Man on third base. When the ball is hit to the left side of the infield, lead off several steps, wait for the throw to first base, then go back to third. If he is extremely fast, the runner should go home on the throw to first base, beating both throws.

When the ball is hit up the middle, go hard for home plate. The infielder moving in toward second base must turn toward home to throw. He will not be able to throw the runner out. Slide hard.

If the ground ball is hit at the second or first baseman, the runner leads off several steps from third base and waits for the throw to first, then retreats back to third. He does not try to score.

Running on Fly Balls

Man on first base. If a short fly ball is hit, go one third of the distance to second base. Stand and watch the ball. Go back to first base if the ball is caught. If the ball is dropped and it bounces far away from the infielder, the runner should be able to slide safely into second base.

On a medium-depth fly ball, go halfway to second base. Stand and watch. Go back to first base if the ball is caught. If the medium fly ball is dropped, the runner should make it safely into second base on a slide.

If a very deep fly ball is hit, run to within 10 to 15 feet of second base. Go back to first base if it is caught. If the ball is dropped, step on second base and be ready to try for third if the ball is far enough out and the fielder has a weak throwing arm.

Man on second base. If a short fly ball is hit, go back to second base. Tag up, stand, and watch. Runner does not attempt to advance to third base.

If the fly ball is of medium depth, go back to second base. When the ball is caught, bluff toward third a couple of steps, and draw a throw to third base. Then retreat back to second base.

When a very deep fly ball is hit, the second-base runner stands on second, watches, and breaks for third after he sees the ball caught. He should go in sliding. If the ball is dropped, the runner might score by the time the ball is thrown in.

Man on third base. If a short fly ball is hit, this is the only exception to the rule of tagging up on third base. In this case, the runner goes down one third of the way toward home, holds his position, and stays ready to move either way. If the ball is caught, he hustles back to third base, sliding if necessary. If the ball is dropped or glances off the fielder's glove, he might score. It depends on his speed.

When a medium fly is hit, the third-base runner will tag up. As the ball is caught, runner will drive hard a few steps toward home, then retreat back to third after the bluff. He does not try to go home.

If a fly ball is very deep, the third-base runner tags up and goes home after the catch. This is the sacrifice fly play. The greatest outfield arm in the world would not be able to throw out a runner of even average speed.

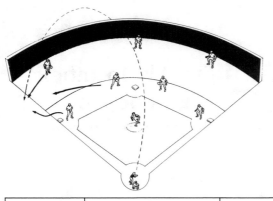

1. Foul Fly to Infield— High Pop-Up to Any Infielder

Runner's situation	Batter does:	Man on 1st does:	Man on 2nd does:	Man on 3rd does:
No one on	Run hard to 1st if fly is close to foul line. Take wide turn at 1st. If fly is fair and dropped, you may be able to go to 2nd.			
Man on 1st	Run hard to 1st if fly is close to foul line. Take wide turn at 1st if 1st-base runner tries for 2nd after the catch.	If fly is deep enough, you might go to 2nd after the catch. Usually you will not. Lead off base, then come back.		
Man on 2nd	Run hard to 1st if fly is close to foul line. Take wide turn at 1st. If runner is on 2nd, stay on 1st.		Tag up.	
Man on 3rd	Same as above ("Man on 2nd").			If fly is deep enough, you might score. Come back to 3rd, tag up, then wait.
Men on 1st and 2nd	Same as "Man on 2nd." Infield fly rule.	Same as above ("Man on 1st").	Tag up.	
Men on 2nd and 3rd	Same as "Man on 2nd."		Tag up.	Same as above ("Man on 3rd").
Men on 1st and 3rd	Same as "Man on 2nd."	Same as "Man on 1st."		Same as "Man on 3rd."
Bases loaded	Same as "Man on 2nd."	Tag up.	Tag up.	Same as "Man on 3rd."

Note. It is assumed in all situations above that there is 0 or 1 out.

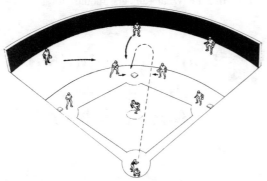

2. Fair Fly to Infield—High Pop-Up to Any Infielder

Runner's situation	Batter does:	Man on 1st does:	Man on 2nd does:	Man on 3rd does:
No one on	Run hard to 1st, round 1st. You might be able to get to 2nd if he drops the ball.			
Man on 1st	Run hard to 1st, round 1st. Stay on 1st if he drops the ball. 2nd is occupied.	Go one third of the way to 2nd. If he drops it, go to 2nd, sliding. If he catches it, go back to 1st.		
Man on 2nd	Same as "No one on."		Tag up.	
Man on 3rd	Same as "No one on."			Get off 3rd base one third of the way. Go back to 3rd if he catches it. Possible to score if he drops ball.
Men on 1st and 2nd	Batter is out. Infield fly rule.	Same as above ("Man on 1st"). Infield fly rule.	Tag up. Infield fly rule.	
Men on 2nd and 3rd	Same as "No one on."		Tag up.	Tag up.
Men on 1st and 3rd	Run hard to 1st, round 1st. You will stay at 1st if 2nd is occupied.	Same as "Man on 1st."		Tag up.
Bases loaded	Infield fly rule.	Tag up. Infield fly rule.	Tag up. Infield fly rule.	Tag up. Infield fly rule.

Note. It is assumed in all situations above that there is 0 or 1 out.

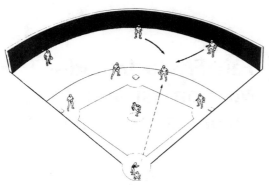

3. Fair Fly to Infield—Hard Line Drive to Infielder

Runner's situation	Batter does:	Man on 1st does:	Man on 2nd does:	Man on 3rd does:
No one on	You are out, but run it out anyway!			
Man on 1st	Same as above.	Dive back to 1st, headfirst.		
Man on 2nd	Same as "No one on."		Dive back to 2nd, headfirst.	
Man on 3rd	Same as "No one on."			Dive back to 3rd, headfirst.
Men on 1st and 2nd	Same as "No one on."	Same as above ("Man on 1st").	Same as above ("Man on 2nd").	
Men on 2nd and 3rd	Same as "No one on."		Same as "Man on 2nd."	Same as above ("Man on 3rd").
Men on 1st and 3rd	Same as "No one on."	Same as "Man on 1st."		Same as "Man on 3rd."
Bases loaded	Same as "No one on."	Same as "Man on 1st."	Same as "Man on 2nd."	Same as "Man on 3rd."

Note. It is assumed in all situations above that there is 0 or 1 out.

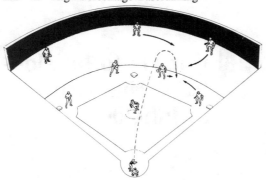

4. Fair Fly to Infield—Men on 1st and 2nd or on 1st, 2nd, and 3rd

Runner's situation	Batter does:	Man on 1st does:	Man on 2nd does:	Man on 3rd does:
No one on	Run to 1st. If fly is dropped, stay on 1st. Automatic out.			
Man on 1st	Same as above.	Infield fly rule does not apply.		
Man on 2nd	Same as "No one on."		Infield fly rule does not apply.	
Man on 3rd	Same as "No one on."			Infield fly rule does not apply.
Men on 1st and 2nd	Same as "No one on."	Stay on your base, whether ball is caught or dropped. Do not run after he drops it, unless it drops deep.	Stay on your base, whether ball is caught or dropped. Do not run after he drops it, unless it drops deep.	
Men on 2nd and 3rd	Same as "No one on."		Same as "Man on 2nd."	Same as above ("Man on 3rd").
Men on 1st and 3rd	Same as "No one on."	Same as "Man on 1st."		Same as "Man on 3rd."
Bases loaded	Same as "No one on."	Stay on your base, whether ball is caught or dropped. Do not run after he drops it.	Stay on your base, whether ball is caught or dropped. Do not run after he drops it.	Stay on your base, whether ball is caught or dropped. Do not run after he drops it.

Note. It is assumed in all situations above that there is 0 or 1 out.

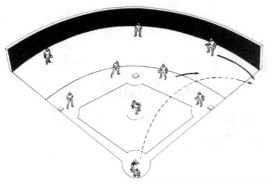

5. Foul Deep Fly to Outfield—Deep to Left-Field or Right-Field Line

Runner's situation	Batter does:	Man on 1st does:	Man on 2nd does:	Man on 3rd does:
No one on	Run hard to 1st if ball is close to foul line. If ball is dropped by right fielder or left fielder, you should be on 2nd. Hustle!			
Man on 1st	Run hard to 1st if ball is close to foul line. If ball is dropped by right fielder or center fielder, stay on 1st. 2nd is occupied.	If foul deep—tag. Go around 2nd—15 ft past it.		
Man on 2nd	Run hard to 1st if ball is close to foul line. If ball is dropped by right fielder or center fielder, you should be on 2nd. Hustle!		Tag up at 2nd. If man catches ball, try for 3rd if you can make it.	
Man on 3rd	Same as above ("Man on 2nd").			Important to tag up! If fly is deep and caught, run after the catch. Slide at home.
Men on 1st and 2nd	Same as "Man on 2nd."	Take lead 10 ft from 2nd. Go to 2nd if fly is fair and dropped. Go back to 1st if caught. If deep, tag.	Same as above ("Man on 2nd").	
Men on 2nd and 3rd	Same as "Man on 2nd."		Same as "Man on 2nd."	Same as above ("Man on 3rd").
Men on 1st and 3rd	Same as "Man on 1st." If deep, get 20 ft from 2nd.	Take lead two thirds of the way to 2nd. Go to 2nd if fly is fair and dropped. Go back to 1st if fly is caught.		Same as "Man on 3rd."
Bases loaded	Same as above ("Men on 1st and 3rd").	Same as "Men on 1st and 3rd." If deep, tag up.	Same as "Man on 2nd."	Same as "Man on 3rd."

Note. It is assumed in all situations above that there is 0 or 1 out.

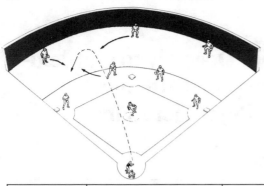

6. Fair Fly to Outfield— Short Fly Caught by Left Fielder, Center Fielder, or Right Fielder

Runner's situation	Batter does:	Man on 1st does:	Man on 2nd does:	Man on 3rd does:
No one on	Run hard to 1st. Round 1st fast. Assume fly will be dropped. Move! End up on 2nd if he drops it!			
Man on 1st	Run hard to 1st. Round 1st fast. Assume fly will be dropped. Go back to 1st if it is dropped.	You are forced. Take a lead one third of distance to 2nd. Don't get "doubled off." Retreat fast to 1st if he catches it. If he drops it, go on to 2nd. Slide.		
Man on 2nd	Same as above ("Man on 1st").		Tag up at 2nd. If fly is dropped, you are not forced to go to 3rd.	
Man on 3rd	Run hard to 1st. Round 1st fast. Assume fly will be dropped. Go to 2nd if it is dropped.			Tag up at 3rd. Watch your 3rd-base coach. If fly is dropped you will score. Slide!
Men on 1st and 2nd	Same as "Man on 1st."	You are forced. Go down one third of distance to 2nd. Get back fast if it is caught. Go fast to 2nd if it is dropped.	You are forced. Tag up at 2nd. If fly is dropped, you must go to 3rd! Slide hard!	
Men on 2nd and 3rd	Run hard to 1st. Round 1st fast. Assume fly will be dropped.		Tag up at 2nd. If fly is dropped, go to 3rd on the throw home.	Tag up at 3rd. If fly is dropped, you will score. Slide!
Men on 1st and 3rd	Same as "Man on 1st."	Same as above ("Men on 1st and 2nd").		Same as above ("Men on 2nd and 3rd").
Bases loaded	Same as "Man on 3rd."	Same as "Men on 1st and 2nd."	You are forced. If fly is dropped, go to 3rd on the throw home.	You are forced. Tag up at 3rd. If fly is dropped, you will score. Slide!

Note. It is assumed in all situations above that there is 0 or 1 out.

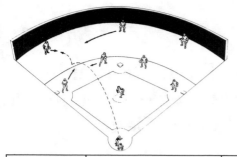

7. Fair Fly to Outfield— Hard Single Over Infield to Left Field

Runner's situation	Batter does:	Man on 1st does:	Man on 2nd does:	Man on 3rd does:
No one on	Run hard down 1st-base line—round 1st and go to 2nd if left fielder bobbles the ball.			
Man on 1st	Run hard down 1st-base line—round 1st and go to 2nd on a bobble if 1st-base runner tries for 3rd.	Run to 2nd and take a wide turn. Advance to 3rd if left fielder bobbles ball badly. Slide hard at 3rd.		
Man on 2nd	Run hard down 1st-base line—round 1st and go to 2nd, sliding if the left fielder's throw goes home.		Run hard to 3rd. Round the bag. Watch 3rd-base coach. Go home sliding if 3rd-base coach waves you home.	
Man on 3rd	Run hard down 1st-base line—round 1st and go to 2nd if left fielder bobbles the ball. If not, retreat back to 1st.			Run hard to home plate. Stand up.
Men on 1st and 2nd	Same as "Man on 1st."	Run to 2nd and take a wide turn. Advance to 3rd if ball is bobbled or if left fielder's throw goes home and 3rd-base runner goes home.	Same as above ("Man on 2nd").	
Men on 2nd and 3rd	Run hard down 1st-base line—round 1st and go to 2nd if ball is bobbled or if left fielder's throw goes home.		Run hard to 3rd. Round the bag. Go home sliding if ball is bobbled or 3rd-base coach waves you home.	Run hard to home plate. Stand up and signal 2nd-base runner coming in to slide or stand up.
Men on 1st and 3rd	Run hard down 1st-base line—round 1st and go to 2nd if ball is bobbled or left fielder's throw goes to 3rd.	Run to 2nd, picking up 3rd-base coach 10 ft before 2nd. Take a wide turn around 2nd. Advance to 3rd. If ball is bobbled or if throw goes to 3rd, go into 3rd sliding.		Same as "Man on 2nd."
Bases loaded	Run hard down 1st-base line—round 1st and go to 2nd on a bobble or a left field throw home if 2nd is vacant.	Run hard to 2nd. If left fielder bobbles ball or throws home and 3rd is vacant, head for 3rd.	Same as above ("Men on 2nd and 3rd").	Same as "Men on 1st and 2nd."

Note. It is assumed in all situations above that there is 0 or 1 out.

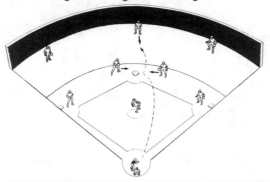

8. Fair Fly to Outfield— Hard Single Over Infield to Center Field

Runner's situation	Batter does:	Man on 1st does:	Man on 2nd does:	Man on 3rd does:
No one on	Run hard to 1st, round 1st, and go to 2nd if center fielder bobbles the ball. If not, retreat to 1st.			
Man on 1st	Run hard to 1st, round 1st, and go to 2nd if center fielder bobbles the ball and 2nd-base runner goes to 3rd.	You are forced. Run to 2nd, round 2nd. Retreat to 2nd on relay in. Go on to 3rd if center fielder bobbles the ball.		
Man on 2nd	Run hard to 1st, round 1st, and go to 2nd if center fielder bobbles the ball or throws home. If not, retreat to 1st.		Break for 3rd, round 3rd. Score if 3rd-base coach waves you on. Slide hard.	
Man on 3rd	Same as "No one on."			Take lead off 3rd. Wait until the hit is sure, then score easily.
Men on 1st and 2nd	Same as "No one on."	You are forced. Run to 2nd, round 2nd. If 3rd-base runner goes in and if center fielder bobbles the ball or throws home, go on to 3rd.	You are forced. Break for 3rd, round 3rd. Score if 3rd-base coach waves you on. Slide hard.	
Men on 2nd and 3rd	Same as "No one on." Center fielder might throw home.		Same as "Man on 2nd."	Same as above ("Man on 3rd"). Signal next runner to stand or slide.
Men on 1st and 3rd	Same as "No one on."	You are forced. Run to 2nd, round 2nd. Go on to 3rd if center fielder bobbles the ball.		Same as "Man on 3rd."
Bases loaded	Same as "Man on 2nd."	You are forced. Run to 2nd, round 2nd. Go on to 3rd if center fielder bobbles the ball or throw comes home. Stay at 2nd if runner is on 3rd.	Same as "Men on 1st and 2nd."	You are forced. Take lead off 3rd. Wait until the hit is sure, then score easily. Signal next runner to stand or slide.

Note. It is assumed in all situations above that there is 0 or 1 out.

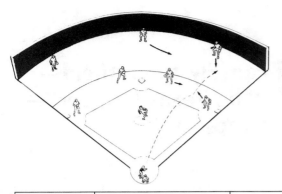

9. Fair Fly to Outfield— Hard Single Over Infield to Right Field

Runner's situation	Batter does:	Man on 1st does:	Man on 2nd does:	Man on 3rd does:
No one on	Run hard to 1st, round 1st, and go to 2nd if right fielder bobbles the ball. If not, retreat to 1st. Take an aggressive turn.			
Man on 1st	Run hard to 1st, round 1st, and go to 2nd if right fielder bobbles the ball and 2nd is vacant. If not, retreat to 1st.	You are forced. Break for 2nd on the hit, pick up 3rd-base coach 10 ft before 2nd, round 2nd. He might wave you on to 3rd.		
Man on 2nd	Run hard to 1st, round 1st, and go to 2nd if right fielder bobbles the ball or throws home. If not, retreat back to 1st. Aggressive turn toward 2nd.		Break for 3rd on the hit. Round 3rd and go in if 3rd-base coach waves you on. Go in sliding hard.	
Man on 3rd	Same as "No one on."			Lead off 3rd. Wait until hit is sure, then score easily.
Men on 1st and 2nd	Run hard to 1st, round 1st, and go to 2nd if right fielder bobbles the ball or throws home.	You are forced. Break for 2nd on the hit, pick up 3rd-base coach 10 ft before 2nd, round 2nd. He might wave you on to 3rd if throw goes home.	You are forced. Break for 3rd on the hit. Round 3rd and go in if 3rd-base coach waves you on. Go in sliding hard.	
Men on 2nd and 3rd	Same as above ("Men on 1st and 2nd").		Same as "Man on 2nd."	Same as above ("Man on 3rd"). Signal next runner to stand or slide.
Men on 1st and 3rd	Same as "Men on 1st and 2nd."	Same as "Man on 1st."		Same as "Man on 3rd."
Bases loaded	Same as "Men on 1st and 2nd."	You are forced. Break for 2nd on the hit. Round 2nd. Watch 3rd-base coach. He might wave you on to 3rd if the throw goes home.	Same as "Men on 1st and 2nd."	You are forced. Lead off 3rd. Wait until the hit is sure. Score easily. Signal next runner whether to stand or slide.

Note. It is assumed in all situations above that there is 0 or 1 out.

10. Fair Fly to Outfield—"The Texas Leaguer"—Drops In

Runner's situation	Batter does:	Man on 1st does:	Man on 2nd does:	Man on 3rd does:
No one on	Run hard to 1st. Round 1st fast and take maximum lead toward 2nd. Retreat back to 1st as relay comes in. Watch for whip play.			
Man on 1st	Run hard to 1st. Round 1st fast and take maximum lead toward 2nd. Retreat back to 1st as relay comes in.	You are forced. Run hard two thirds of the way toward 2nd. Make sure it drops in. Go on to 2nd on the hit. Stay at 2nd.		
Man on 2nd	Same as above ("Man on 1st").		Take good lead off 2nd. Watch until ball drops in for the hit. Go on to 3rd and slide. Stay at 3rd.	
Man on 3rd	Same as "Man on 1st."			Tag up. Watch until ball drops in for the hit. Go on home and score.
Men on 1st and 2nd	Same as "Man on 1st."	Same as above ("Man on 1st").	You are forced. Take good lead off 2nd. Watch until ball drops in for a hit. Go on to 3rd and slide. Stay at 3rd.	
Men on 2nd and 3rd	Same as "Man on 1st."		Same as "Man on 2nd."	Same as above ("Man on 3rd").
Men on 1st and 3rd	Same as "Man on 1st."	Same as "Man on 1st."		Same as "Man on 3rd."
Bases loaded	Same as "Man on 1st."	Same as "Man on 1st."	Same as "Men on 1st and 2nd."	You are forced. Tag up. Watch until ball drops in for the hit. Go on home and score.

Note. It is assumed in all situations above that there is 0 or 1 out.

11. Fair Fly to Outfield— Power Alley Hit— Bounce to the Fence

Runner's situation	Batter does:	Man on 1st does:	Man on 2nd does:	Man on 3rd does:
No one on	You know you can make 2nd. Pick up the 3rd-base coach 10 ft before 2nd. If you go to 3rd, slide hard.			
Man on 1st	Same as above.	You are forced. Go down to within 10 ft of 2nd. Stand. Pick up the 3rd-base coach. Watch until ball goes between the outfielders. You will score easily.		
Man on 2nd	Same as "No one on."		Tag up. Stay on 2nd. Watch ball until it goes between outfielders. You will score easily. Do not slide.	
Man on 3rd	Same as "No one on."			Tag up. Stay on 3rd until ball goes between the outfielders. Score easily.
Men on 1st and 2nd	You know you can make 2nd. Round 1st fast, go for 2nd.	You are forced. Go down to within 10 ft of 2nd. Stand. Watch until ball goes between the outfielders. You will score easily. Slide anyway.	You are forced. Tag up at 2nd. Watch ball until it goes between the outfielders. Score. Signal next runner to stand or slide.	
Men on 2nd and 3rd	You know you can make 2nd. Go for 3rd. Round 1st fast, round 2nd. Now watch 3rd-base coach. If you go to 3rd, slide hard.		Tag up at 2nd. Watch ball until it goes between the outfielders. Score. Slide.	Tag up. Stay on 3rd until ball goes between the outfielders. Score easily. Signal next runner to stand or slide.
Men on 1st and 3rd	Same as above ("Men on 2nd and 3rd").	You are forced. Go down to within 10 ft of 2nd. Stand. Pick up the 3rd-base coach. Watch until ball goes between the outfielders. You will score. Slide anyway.		Same as above ("Men on 2nd and 3rd").
Bases loaded	You know you can make 2nd. Go for 3rd.	Same as above ("Men on 1st and 3rd").	You are forced. Tag up at 2nd. Watch ball until it goes between the outfielders. Score. Slide. Signal runner to stand or slide.	You are forced. Tag up. Stay on 3rd until it goes between the outfielders. Score easily. Signal runners to stand or slide.

Note. It is assumed in all situations above that there is 0 or 1 out.

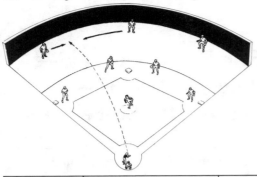

12. Fair Fly to Outfield— Deep Fly Caught by Left Fielder, Center Fielder, or Right Fielder

Runner's situation	Batter does:	Man on 1st does:	Man on 2nd does:	Man on 3rd does:
No one on	Run hard to 1st. Round 1st and go at least half-way to 2nd. If fly is dropped, round 2nd. You might get to 3rd.			
Man on 1st	Same as above.	You are forced. Run down 10 ft from 2nd. If the fly is dropped, end up on 3rd. Slide at 3rd. Watch 3rd-base coach's sign. Retreat to 1st if caught.		
Man on 2nd	Same as "No one on."		Tag up at 2nd. If he catches it, go on to 3rd. If he drops it, break for 3rd. Watch 3rd-base coach. He may wave you on to score.	
Man on 3rd	Same as "No one on." If outfield throw is not caught, go to 2nd.			Tag up at 3rd. Go home and score after the catch. Slide! Score if he drops it.
Men on 1st and 2nd	Same as "No one on."	Same as above ("Man on 1st").	You are forced. Tag up. If he catches it, go on to 3rd, sliding. If he drops it, break for 3rd. Slide. Watch 3rd-base coach.	
Men on 2nd and 3rd	Same as "No one on."		Tag up at 2nd. If he catches it, go to 3rd, sliding. If he drops it, break for 3rd. Slide. Watch 3rd-base coach.	Same as above ("Man on 3rd").
Men on 1st and 3rd	Same as "No one on."	Same as "Man on 1st."		Same as "Man on 3rd."
Bases loaded	Run hard to 1st. Round 1st and go at least half-way to 2nd. If fly is dropped, go back to 1st.	Go halfway down to 2nd.	Same as "Men on 1st and 2nd."	You are forced. Tag up at 3rd. Go home and score after the catch. Score if he drops it.

Note. It is assumed in all situations above that there is 0 or 1 out.

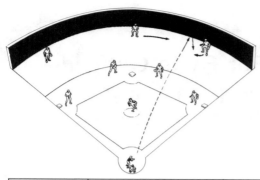

13. Fair Fly to Outfield—Hit Top of Fence—Bounce Back

Runner's situation	Batter does:	Man on 1st does:	Man on 2nd does:	Man on 3rd does:
No one on	Never slow down as you run to 1st. Assume it is a double off the wall. Stretch it to a triple if 3rd is vacant. Then move and slide.			
Man on 1st	Same as above.	You are forced. Go down 10 ft beyond 1st. Stay there until ball bounces off the wall. You will reach 3rd easily. Maybe you can score.		
Man on 2nd	Same as "No one on."		Tag up. Stay on 2nd. If ball bounces back, you should score. Slide!	
Man on 3rd	Same as "No one on."			Tag up. Stay on 3rd. You will score easily as the ball bounces off wall.
Men on 1st and 2nd	Same as "No one on."	You are forced. Go down to within 10 ft of 2nd. Stay there until ball bounces off the wall. You will reach 3rd easily. Slide!	You are forced. Tag up. Stay on 2nd. If ball bounces back, you should score. Slide!	
Men on 2nd and 3rd	Same as "No one on."		Same as "Man on 2nd."	Same as above ("Man on 3rd"). Signal next runner to stand or slide.
Men on 1st and 3rd	Same as "No one on."	You are forced. Go down 10 ft beyond 2nd. Stay there until ball bounces off the wall. You will reach 3rd easily. Score!		Same as "Man on 3rd."
Bases loaded	Same as "No one on."	Same as "Men on 1st and 2nd."	Same as "Men on 1st and 2nd."	You are forced. Tag up. Stay on 3rd. You will score easily as the ball bounces off the wall. Signal next runner to stand or slide.

Note.   It is assumed in all situations above that there is 0 or 1 out.

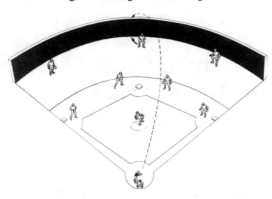

14. Fair Fly to Outfield— Deep Fly Caught Against Fence

Runner's situation	Batter does:	Man on 1st does:	Man on 2nd does:	Man on 3rd does:
No one on	Never slow down as you run to 1st. Assume it is a double off the wall. Should be 15 ft from 2nd when ball is caught.			
Man on 1st	Same as above.	Go to within 10 ft of 2nd.		
Man on 2nd	Same as "No one on."		Tag up at 2nd. Watch fly until it is caught. Go to 3rd hard if you are fast enough. Slide hard.	
Man on 3rd	Same as "No one on."			Tag up at 3rd. Watch fly until it is caught. Score easily. Don't slide.
Men on 1st and 2nd	Same as "No one on."	You are forced. Go down to within 10 ft of 2nd. Stand. Watch the catch. Retreat back to 1st. Tag up.	You are forced. Tag up at 2nd. Watch fly until it is caught. Go to 3rd hard if you are fast enough. Slide hard.	
Men on 2nd and 3rd	Same as "No one on."		Same as above ("Men on 1st and 2nd").	Same as above ("Man on 3rd").
Men on 1st and 3rd	Same as "No one on."	Go to within 10 ft of 2nd.		Same as "Man on 3rd."
Bases loaded	Same as "No one on."	Go to within 10 ft of 2nd.	Same as "Men on 1st and 2nd."	You are forced. Tag up at 3rd. Watch fly until it is caught. Score easily. Don't slide.

Note. It is assumed in all situations above that there is 0 or 1 out.

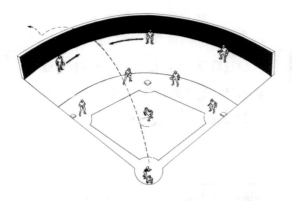

15. Fair Fly to Outfield—"The Sure Home Run"

Runner's situation	Batter does:	Man on 1st does:	Man on 2nd does:	Man on 3rd does:
No one on	Never slow down as you run to 1st. Assume it is a double off the wall. Move!*			
Man on 1st	Same as above.	You are forced. Go down to 10 ft beyond 2nd. Watch the ball. You should be on 3rd if the ball bounces back.		
Man on 2nd	Same as "No one on."		Tag up. Stay on 2nd. If ball is a home run or bounces back, you should score. Slide.	
Man on 3rd	Same as "No one on."			Tag up. Stay on 3rd. If ball is a home run or bounces back, you should score.
Men on 1st and 2nd	Same as "No one on."	You are forced. Go down to within 10 ft of 2nd. Watch the ball. You should be on 3rd if the ball bounces back.	You are forced. Tag up. Stay on 2nd. If ball is a home run or bounces back, you should score. Slide.	
Men on 2nd and 3rd	Same as "No one on."		Same as "Man on 2nd."	Same as above ("Man on 3rd"). Signal next runner to stand or slide.
Men on 1st and 3rd	Same as "No one on."	Same as above ("Men on 1st and 2nd").		Same as "Man on 3rd."
Bases loaded	Same as "No one on."	Same as "Men on 1st and 2nd." Tag upon deep fly.	Same as "Men on 1st and 2nd."	You are forced. Tag up. Stay on 3rd. If ball is a home run or bounces back, you should score. Signal next runner to slide or stand.

Note. It is assumed in all situations above that there is 0 or 1 out.

*The man who hits the "sure home run" should be near 2nd by the time the high home run clears the fence. Really move!

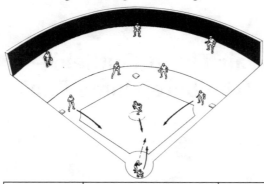

16. Ground Ball to Infield— Weak Grounder— Catcher Fields It

Runner's situation	Batter does:	Man on 1st does:	Man on 2nd does:	Man on 3rd does:
No one on	Run hard to 1st. Run down the line. Overthrow will go into right field. Head for 2nd on the overthrow. Maybe go to 3rd.			
Man on 1st	Run hard to 1st. Run down the line. Overthrow will go into right field. Head for 2nd on the overthrow.	You are forced. Break for 2nd fast. Slide hard. Break up the double play at 2nd.		
Man on 2nd	Same as above ("Man on 1st").		Hold your lead off 2nd. When catcher throws to 1st, break hard for 3rd. Slide hard.	
Man on 3rd	Same as "Man on 1st."			Take some lead off 3rd. When catcher throws to 1st, be ready to score on an overthrow.
Men on 1st and 2nd	Same as "Man on 1st."	Same as above ("Man on 1st").	You are forced. Break for 3rd. Slide hard. Break up the 3rd-to-1st double play.	
Men on 2nd and 3rd	Same as "Man on 1st."		Hold your lead off 2nd. When catcher throws to 1st, stay at 2nd.	Same as above ("Man on 3rd").
Men on 1st and 3rd	Same as "Man on 1st."	Same as "Man on 1st."		Take some lead off 3rd. When catcher throws to 2nd, be ready to score on a double play attempt.
Bases loaded	Same as "Man on 1st."	Same as "Man on 1st."	Same as "Men on 1st and 2nd."	You are forced. Break for home and try to cause bad catcher's throw at 1st, which scores 2 runs.

Note. It is assumed in all situations above that there is 0 or 1 out.

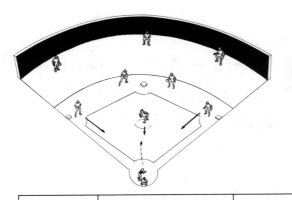

17. Ground Ball to Infield— Slow Grounder to Pitcher

Runner's situation	Batter does:	Man on 1st does:	Man on 2nd does:	Man on 3rd does:
No one on	Run hard to 1st. Run down the line. On an overthrow at 1st, turn in and go to 2nd, sliding.			
Man on 1st	Same as above.	You are forced. Break for 2nd and go in sliding. Break up the 2nd-to-1st double play.		
Man on 2nd	Same as "No one on."		Get a good lead off 2nd. Go to 3rd if you have the lead and speed. Otherwise, hold your lead, then go back to 2nd.	
Man on 3rd	Same as "No one on."			Take good lead off 3rd. Bluff going home quickly. Then go back to 3rd.
Men on 1st and 2nd	Same as "No one on."	Same as above ("Man on 1st").	You are forced. Break for 3rd. Go in sliding. Break up the 3rd-to-1st double play.	
Men on 2nd and 3rd	Same as "No one on."		Get a good lead off 2nd. Go to 3rd if you have the lead and speed and if 3rd-base runner tries for home.	Take good lead off 3rd. Bluff going home. Go home if you have the lead and speed, as pitcher throws to 1st or 2nd.
Men on 1st and 3rd	Same as "No one on."	Same as "Man on 1st."		Take good lead off 3rd. Bluff going home. Go home if you have the lead and speed, or if pitcher goes to 2nd for a double play.
Bases loaded	Same as "No one on."	Same as "Man on 1st."	Same as "Men on 1st and 2nd."	You are forced. Go home hard and slide. Break up home-to-1st double play.

Note. It is assumed in all situations above that there is 0 or 1 out.

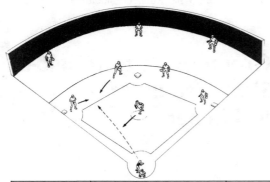

18. Ground Ball to Infield—Slow Grounder to 3rd, Shortstop, 2nd, or 1st

Runner's situation	Batter does:	Man on 1st does:	Man on 2nd does:	Man on 3rd does:
No one on	Run hard to 1st. Run down the line. On an overthrow at 1st, turn in and go to 2nd, sliding.			
Man on 1st	Same as above.	You are forced. Break for 2nd and slide hard. Break up the 2nd-to-1st double play.		
Man on 2nd	Same as "No one on."		If grounder is to 2nd or 1st, break for 3rd and slide. If grounder is to the shortstop or 3rd, only a fast man can go to 3rd.	
Man on 3rd	Same as "No one on."			Take good lead off 3rd. Bluff going home. Go home only if you have the lead and speed.
Men on 1st and 2nd	Same as "No one on."	Same as above ("Man on 1st").	You are forced. Break for 3rd fast. Slide hard. Try to break up the 3rd-to-1st double play.	
Men on 2nd and 3rd	Same as "No one on."		If grounder is to 2nd or 1st, and 3rd is vacant, break for 3rd and slide. Only a fast man can do this if the ball is to the shortstop or 3rd.	Same as above ("Man on 3rd").
Men on 1st and 3rd	Same as "No one on."	Same as "Man on 1st."		Same as "Man on 3rd."
Bases loaded	Same as "No one on."	Same as "Man on 1st."	Same as "Men on 1st and 2nd."	You are forced. Break for home fast. Try to break up the home-to-1st double play. Slide hard.

Note. It is assumed in all situations above that there is 0 or 1 out.

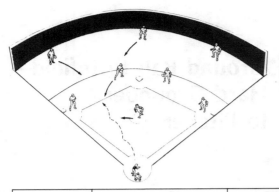

19. Ground Ball to Infield— High Chopper to Any Infielder

Runner's situation	Batter does:	Man on 1st does:	Man on 2nd does:	Man on 3rd does:
No one on	Run very hard to 1st. Runner might get a base hit off a high chopper. Run down the line. React to an overthrow.			
Man on 1st	Same as above.	You are forced. Run hard to 2nd, slide hard. You could beat out a double play on a high chopper.		
Man on 2nd	Same as "No one on."		Go if ball is hit to 2nd or 1st. On a high chopper, the infielder doesn't have much time. If ball is hit to the shortstop or 3rd, advance with caution.	
Man on 3rd	Same as "No one on."			Break for home. On a high chopper you should score. Slide hard. Read the play and the bounce of the ball.
Men on 1st and 2nd	Same as "No one on."	Same as above ("Man on 1st").	You are forced. Break for 3rd with the hit. Slide hard. Break up a 3rd-to-1st double play.	
Men on 2nd and 3rd	Same as "No one on."		Go if ball is hit to 2nd or 1st and 3rd-base runner advances. Otherwise, stay on 2nd.	Same as above ("Man on 3rd").
Men on 1st and 3rd	Same as "No one on."	Same as "Man on 1st."		Same as "Man on 3rd."
Bases loaded	Same as "No one on."	Same as "Man on 1st."	Same as "Men on 1st and 2nd."	You are forced. Break for home. Slide hard. Make catcher overthrow at 1st. This scores 2 runs for you.

Note. It is assumed in all situations above that there is 0 or 1 out.

20. Ground Ball to Infield— Hard Grounder to Pitcher

Runner's situation	Batter does:	Man on 1st does:	Man on 2nd does:	Man on 3rd does:
No one on	Run hard to 1st. Run down the line. On an overthrow at 1st, turn in and head for 2nd. Slide.			
Man on 1st	Same as above.	You are forced. Break for 2nd at the crack of the bat. Slide hard. Break up the 2nd-to-1st double play.		
Man on 2nd	Same as "No one on."		Hold your position. Take a good lead off 2nd. Go to 3rd if pitcher overthrows at 1st.	
Man on 3rd	Same as "No one on."			Take a step or two back toward 3rd. Hold the position. Score if pitcher overthrows at 2nd or 1st.
Men on 1st and 2nd	Same as "No one on."	Same as above ("Man on 1st").	You are forced. Break at the crack of the bat. Slide hard to break up the 3rd-to-1st double play.	
Men on 2nd and 3rd	Same as "No one on."		Same as "Man on 2nd."	Same as above ("Man on 3rd").
Men on 1st and 3rd	Same as "No one on."	Same as "Man on 1st."		Same as "Man on 3rd." Also score if they try double play at 2nd.
Bases loaded	Same as "No one on."	Same as "Man on 1st."	Same as "Men on 1st and 2nd."	You are forced. Break for home at the crack of the bat. Slide hard to break up the home-to-1st double play.

Note. It is assumed in all situations above that there is 0 or 1 out.

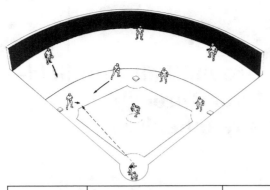

21. Ground Ball to Infield— Hard Grounder to 3rd, Shortstop, 2nd, or 1st

Runner's situation	Batter does:	Man on 1st does:	Man on 2nd does:	Man on 3rd does:
No one on	Run hard to 1st. Run down the line. On an overthrow at 1st, turn in and head for 2nd. Slide hard.			
Man on 1st	Same as above.	You are forced. Go hard to 2nd and take out the 2nd baseman or shortstop, breaking up the double play.		
Man on 2nd	Same as "No one on."		If grounder is to shortstop or 3rd, do not advance to 3rd unless ball is overthrown at 1st. You may advance on ball hit to 2nd or 1st.	
Man on 3rd	Same as "No one on."			Hold your position. Do not score unless ball is overthrown at 2nd or 1st.
Men on 1st and 2nd	Same as "No one on."	You are forced. Break for 2nd. Slide hard. Break up the 2nd-to-1st double play.	You are forced. Break for 3rd. Slide hard. Break up the 3rd-to-1st double play.	
Men on 2nd and 3rd	Same as "No one on."		Do not advance to 3rd unless a throw goes to home plate or there is an overthrow.	Hold your position. Do not score unless ball is overthrown at 2nd or 1st.
Men on 1st and 3rd	Same as "No one on."	Same as above ("Men on 1st and 2nd").		Same as above ("Men on 2nd and 3rd"). Also score on a double play at 2nd.
Bases loaded	Same as "No one on."	Same as "Men on 1st and 2nd."	Same as "Men on 1st and 2nd."	You are forced. Break for the plate. Slide hard. Try to make catcher overthrow at 1st. This scores 2 runs!

Note. It is assumed in all situations above that there is 0 or 1 out.

22. Ground Ball to Infield— Error Through Any Infielder

Runner's situation	Batter does:	Man on 1st does:	Man on 2nd does:	Man on 3rd does:
No one on	Run hard to 1st, down the line to beat out the throw. Turn into infield. Probably can't go to 2nd, unless the ball veers off infielder.			
Man on 1st	Run hard to 1st, down the line to beat out the throw. Turn into infield. Probably can't go to 2nd.	You are forced. Must go at the crack of the bat. On the error, take turn at 2nd. Perhaps can go to 3rd—watch 3rd-base coach.		
Man on 2nd	Same as above.		You are not forced. If ball is hit to 1st, 2nd, 3rd, or the shortstop, hold up until error is made.	
Man on 3rd	Same as "Man on 1st."			You are not forced. On a hard-hit ball, hold up until error is made. On a slow roller, head home and slide.
Men on 1st and 2nd	Same as "Man on 1st."	Same as above ("Man on 1st").	You are forced. Must go at the crack of the bat. After error, round 3rd—go home if 3rd-base coach waves you in.	
Men on 2nd and 3rd	Same as "Man on 1st."		You are not forced. If ball is hit to shortstop or 3rd, hold up until error is made. Go to 3rd if 3rd-base runner goes home.	Same as above ("Man on 3rd").
Men on 1st and 3rd	Same as "Man on 1st."	Same as "Man on 1st."		Same as "Man on 3rd."
Bases loaded	Same as "Man on 1st."	Same as "Man on 1st."	You are forced. Go at the crack of the bat. Take turn at 3rd. Maybe can go home. Watch 3rd-base coach.	You are forced. Go at the crack of the bat. Signal next runner coming in to slide or stand.

Note. It is assumed in all situations above that there is 0 or 1 out.

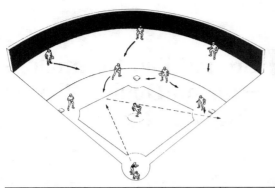

23. Ground Ball to Infield— Error on Throw Over 1st

Runner's situation	Batter does:	Man on 1st does:	Man on 2nd does:	Man on 3rd does:
No one on	Run hard to 1st. Run down the line. If ball is overthrown, turn in and head for 2nd.			
Man on 1st	Same as above.	You are forced. Go at the crack of the bat. Slide hard. Break up the double play at 2nd.		
Man on 2nd	Same as "No one on."		If you broke for 3rd as ball was hit to right side of infield, you should score on the overthrow. Hold up on grounder to left side.	
Man on 3rd	Same as "No one on."			Take some lead off 3rd. As the ball is overthrown at 1st, score easily.
Men on 1st and 2nd	Same as "No one on."	Same as above ("Man on 1st").	You are forced. Break for 3rd as ball is hit. Slide hard to beat the 3rd-to-1st double play.	
Men on 2nd and 3rd	Same as "No one on."		If you broke for 3rd as ball was hit to right side of infield, you should score on the overthrow.	Same as above ("Man on 3rd").
Men on 1st and 3rd	Same as "No one on."	Same as "Man on 1st."		Same as "Man on 3rd."
Bases loaded	Same as "No one on."	Same as "Man on 1st."	Same as "Men on 1st and 2nd."	You are forced. Go home hard on the hit. Take out the catcher, force a bad throw at 1st. Signal next runner in to slide or stand.

Note. It is assumed in all situations above that there is 0 or 1 out.

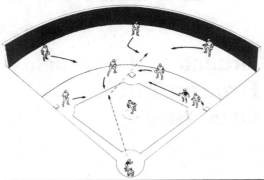

24. Ground Ball to Infield— Error on Double Play Throw at 2nd

Runner's situation	Batter does:	Man on 1st does:	Man on 2nd does:	Man on 3rd does:
No one on	Impossible situation.			
Man on 1st	Run down to 1st. Run down the line. If ball is overthrown at 2nd, take turn in. Go to 2nd if it is vacant and you can make it.	You are forced. Go at the crack of the bat. Slide hard to break up the double play. Go to 3rd on the overthrow.		
Man on 2nd	Impossible situation.		Impossible situation.	
Man on 3rd	Impossible situation.			Impossible situation.
Men on 1st and 2nd	Same as "Man on 1st."	Same as above ("Man on 1st").	You are forced. Break for 3rd and slide to prevent 3rd-to-1st double play. Go home on the overthrow.	
Men on 2nd and 3rd	Impossible situation.		Impossible situation.	Impossible situation.
Men on 1st and 3rd	Same as "Man on 1st."	Same as "Man on 1st."		Take a lead off 3rd. Hold the lead. Go home as ball is overthrown at 2nd.
Bases loaded	Same as "Man on 1st."	Same as "Man on 1st."	You are forced. Go at the crack of the bat. Break for 3rd and slide to prevent 3rd-to-1st double play. Go home on the overthrow.	You are forced. Go at the crack of the bat. Slide hard. Signal next runner to slide or stand.

Note. It is assumed in all situations above that there is 0 or 1 out.

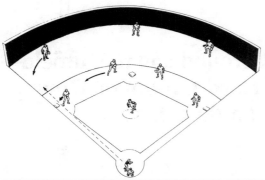

25. Ground Ball to Outfield— Hard Grounder Down 3rd-Base Line

Runner's situation	Batter does:	Man on 1st does:	Man on 2nd does:	Man on 3rd does:
No one on	Run hard to 1st. Round 1st and head for 2nd if 1st-base coach waves you on. Slide hard at 2nd.			
Man on 1st	Same as above.	You are forced. Run hard for 2nd. Round 2nd and head for 3rd if 3rd-base coach waves you on. Slide hard at 3rd.		
Man on 2nd	Same as "No one on."		Run hard to 3rd, round the base, and go into home sliding.	
Man on 3rd	Same as "No one on."			Score easily on the base hit.
Men on 1st and 2nd	Same as "No one on."	Same as above ("Man on 1st").	You are forced. Run hard to 3rd, round the base, and go into home sliding.	
Men on 2nd and 3rd	Same as "No one on."		Same as "Man on 2nd."	Score easily on the base hit. Signal next runner to stand or slide.
Men on 1st and 3rd	Same as "No one on."	Same as "Man on 1st."		Score easily on the base hit.
Bases loaded	Same as "No one on."	Same as "Man on 1st."	Same as "Men on 1st and 2nd."	Same as "Men on 2nd and 3rd."

Note. It is assumed in all situations above that there is 0 or 1 out.

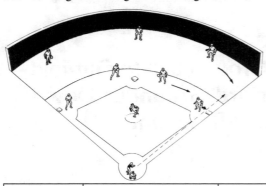

26. Ground Ball to Outfield— Hard Grounder Down 1st-Base Line

Runner's situation	Batter does:	Man on 1st does:	Man on 2nd does:	Man on 3rd does:
No one on	Run hard to 1st and head for 2nd. Take turn at 2nd and watch 3rd-base coach. You might make it to 3rd.			
Man on 1st	Run hard to 1st and head for 2nd. Take turn at 2nd and watch 3rd-base coach. You might make it to 3rd if right fielder throws home.	You are forced. Run hard around 2nd and into 3rd. Round 3rd and go home if 3rd-base coach waves you in.		
Man on 2nd	Run hard to 1st and head for 2nd. Take turn at 2nd and go to 3rd if the coach waves you on.		Go hard on the hit. Round 3rd and go home, sliding.	
Man on 3rd	Same as above ("Man on 2nd").			Score easily on the base hit over 1st.
Men on 1st and 2nd	Same as "Man on 2nd."	Same as above ("Man on 1st").	You are forced. Go hard on the hit. Round 3rd and go home, sliding. Signal next runner to slide or stand.	
Men on 2nd and 3rd	Same as "Man on 2nd."		Same as "Man on 2nd."	Score easily on the base hit over 1st and signal next runner to slide or stand.
Men on 1st and 3rd	Same as "Man on 2nd."	Same as "Man on 1st."		Same as above ("Men on 2nd and 3rd").
Bases loaded	Same as "Man on 2nd."	Same as "Man on 1st."	Same as "Men on 1st and 2nd."	Same as "Men on 2nd and 3rd."

Note. It is assumed in all situations above that there is 0 or 1 out.

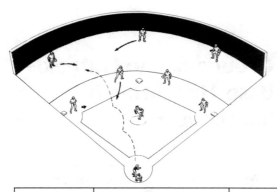

27. Ground Ball to Outfield— High Chopper Over Infield

Runner's situation	Batter does:	Man on 1st does:	Man on 2nd does:	Man on 3rd does:
No one on	Run down the line and take the wide turn at 1st. Advance to 2nd if the ball is bobbled by the outfielder.			
Man on 1st	Run down the line and take the wide turn at 1st. Advance to 2nd on a bobbled ball if 2nd-base runner tries for 3rd.	Run to 2nd. Take a good turn at 2nd and advance to 3rd if the ball is bobbled by the outfielder.		
Man on 2nd	Run down the line and take the wide turn at 1st. If the outfielder bobbles the ball or throws home, head for 2nd.		Run to 3rd and watch the 3rd-base coach's sign. Take a wide turn at 3rd and score if you are waved in.	
Man on 3rd	Same as "No one on."			Take a good lead off 3rd. Head for home as soon as ball hops over infielder's head.
Men on 1st and 2nd	Same as "Man on 2nd."	Run to 2nd. Take a good turn at 2nd and advance to 3rd if the ball is bobbled or thrown home.	Run to 3rd on the hit ball and take a big turn. Watch the 3rd-base coach's sign. Score if you are waved in.	
Men on 2nd and 3rd	Same as "Man on 2nd."		Same as above ("Men on 1st and 2nd").	Score on the hit as soon as you see it hop over the infielder.
Men on 1st and 3rd	Same as "Man on 2nd."	Same as "Man on 1st."		Same as above ("Men on 2nd and 3rd").
Bases loaded	Same as "Man on 2nd."	Same as "Men on 1st and 2nd."	Be on your way to 3rd on the ground ball and score easily after it hops over the infielder.	Same as "Men on 2nd and 3rd."

Note. It is assumed in all situations above that there is 0 or 1 out.

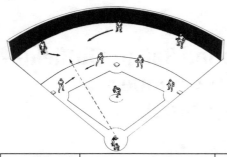

28. Ground Ball to Outfield— Base Hit Through Shortstop Hole

Runner's situation	Batter does:	Man on 1st does:	Man on 2nd does:	Man on 3rd does:
No one on	Run hard to 1st, round 1st with a big lead. Be ready to go to 2nd if left fielder bobbles the ball.			
Man on 1st	Run hard to 1st, round 1st with a big lead. Be ready to go to 2nd if it is vacant and left fielder bobbles the ball.	You are forced. Run hard to 2nd and round 2nd. Be ready to go to 3rd if left fielder bobbles the ball.		
Man on 2nd	Run hard to 1st, round 1st with a big lead. Be ready to go to 2nd if left fielder bobbles the ball or throws home.		Run hard to 3rd. Make turn at 3rd. Keep going home if 3rd-base coach waves you on.	
Man on 3rd	Same as "No one on."			Score easily on the base hit.
Men on 1st and 2nd	Same as "Man on 2nd."	You are forced. Run hard to 2nd and round 2nd. Be ready to go to 3rd if left fielder bobbles the ball or left fielder's throw goes home.	You are forced. Run hard to 3rd. Make turn at 3rd. Keep going home if 3rd-base coach waves you on.	
Men on 2nd and 3rd	Same as "Man on 2nd."		Same as "Man on 2nd."	Score easily on the base hit and signal next runner to slide or stand.
Men on 1st and 3rd	Same as "Man on 2nd."	Same as "Man on 1st."		Same as "Man on 3rd."
Bases loaded	Same as "Man on 2nd."	Same as "Men on 1st and 2nd."	Same as "Men on 1st and 2nd."	Same as "Men on 2nd and 3rd."

Note. It is assumed in all situations above that there is 0 or 1 out.

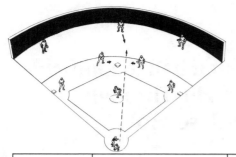

29. Ground Ball to Outfield— Base Hit Up the Middle

Runner's situation	Batter does:	Man on 1st does:	Man on 2nd does:	Man on 3rd does:
No one on	Run hard to 1st, take a wide turn toward 2nd. Be alert to go to 2nd if center fielder bobbles the ball or if it goes through him.			
Man on 1st	Run hard to 1st, take a wide turn toward 2nd. Be alert to go to 2nd if center fielder bobbles ball and 1st-base runner advances.	You are forced. Run hard to 2nd and take a lead off 2nd. Head for 3rd if center fielder bobbles the ball or misses it.		
Man on 2nd	Same as "No one on."		You are not forced, but run hard to 3rd and take turn. Head home and slide if 3rd-base coach waves you home.	
Man on 3rd	Same as "No one on."			Score on the base hit. No need to slide.
Men on 1st and 2nd	Run hard to 1st, take a wide turn toward 2nd. Be alert to go to 2nd if center fielder bobbles the ball or if throw goes home.	You are forced. Run hard to 2nd and take a lead off 2nd. Head for 3rd if center fielder bobbles the ball or if throw goes home.	You are forced. Run hard to 3rd and take turn. Head home and slide if 3rd-base coach waves you home.	
Men on 2nd and 3rd	Same as "No one on."		Same as "Man on 2nd."	You are not forced. Score on the base hit. No need to slide. Signal next runner to stand or slide.
Men on 1st and 3rd	Same as "No one on."	You are forced. Run hard to 2nd and take a lead off 2nd. Head for 3rd if center fielder bobbles the ball or if it goes through him.		You are not forced. Score on the base hit. No need to slide.
Bases loaded	Same as "Men on 1st and 2nd."	You are forced. Run hard to 2nd and take a turn. Head for 3rd if center fielder bobbles ball or if throw goes home.	Same as "Men on 1st and 2nd."	You are forced. Go hard off 3rd and do not slide. Signal next runner to stand or slide.

Note. It is assumed in all situations above that there is 0 or 1 out.

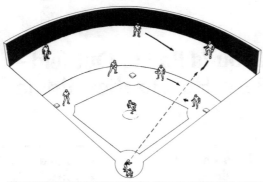

30. Ground Ball to Outfield— Base Hit Through 2nd-Base Hole

Runner's situation	Batter does:	Man on 1st does:	Man on 2nd does:	Man on 3rd does:
No one on	Run hard to 1st. Round 1st and be ready to go to 2nd if right fielder bobbles the ball.			
Man on 1st	Same as above.	You are forced. Run hard to 2nd and take a wide turn. Be ready to go to 3rd if right fielder bobbles the ball.		
Man on 2nd	Run hard to 1st. Round 1st and be ready to go to 2nd if right fielder bobbles the ball or throws to home.		Go hard to 3rd and round 3rd. Keep going home if 3rd-base coach waves you home. Slide at home.	
Man on 3rd	Same as "No one on."			Score easily on the base hit.
Men on 1st and 2nd	Same as "Man on 2nd."	You are forced. Run hard to 2nd and take a wide turn. Be ready to go to 3rd if the runner there goes home.	You are forced. Go hard to 3rd and round 3rd. Keep going home if 3rd-base coach waves you home. Slide at home.	
Men on 2nd and 3rd	Same as "Man on 2nd."		Same as "Man on 2nd."	Score easily on the base hit. Signal next runner to slide or stand.
Men on 1st and 3rd	Same as "Man on 2nd."	Same as "Man on 1st."		Score easily on the base hit.
Bases loaded	Same as "Man on 2nd."	Same as "Man on 1st."	Same as "Men on 1st and 2nd."	You are forced. Score easily on the base hit and signal next runner to slide or stand.

Note. It is assumed in all situations above that there is 0 or 1 out.

31. Bunted Ball in the Air— Ball May Be Caught by Infield

Runner's situation	Batter does:	Man on 1st does:	Man on 2nd does:	Man on 3rd does:
No one on	Run hard to 1st. If bunt fly is dropped, stay on 1st.			
Man on 1st	Same as above.	Take small lead off 1st. If bunt fly is caught, go back to 1st. If fly is dropped, run to 2nd.		
Man on 2nd	Same as "No one on."		Take small lead off 2nd. If bunt fly is caught or dropped and 3rd is covered, go back to 2nd.	
Man on 3rd	Same as "No one on."			Take small lead off 3rd. Go back to 3rd whether bunt fly is caught or dropped.
Men on 1st and 2nd	Same as "No one on."	Same as above ("Man on 1st").	Same as above ("Man on 2nd").	
Men on 2nd and 3rd	Same as "No one on."		Take small lead off 2nd. Go back to 2nd whether bunt fly is caught or dropped.	Same as above ("Man on 3rd").
Men on 1st and 3rd	Same as "No one on."	Same as "Man on 1st."		Same as "Man on 3rd."
Bases loaded	Same as "No one on."	Take small lead off 1st. If bunt fly is caught, go back to 1st. If fly is dropped, run to 2nd fast. Prevent double play or force play.	If bunt fly is dropped, you have to go to next base fast. Prevent double play or force play.	If bunt fly is dropped, you have to go to next base fast. Prevent double play or force play.

Note. It is assumed in all situations above that there is 0 or 1 out.

32. Bunted Ball— Slow Roller— Catcher Fields It

Runner's situation	Batter does:	Man on 1st does:	Man on 2nd does:	Man on 3rd does:
No one on	Run hard to 1st. Be sure to stay outside the line. Do not take the turn.			
Man on 1st	Same as above.	You are forced. Run hard to 2nd and slide to prevent the catcher-to-2nd-to-1st double play.		
Man on 2nd	Same as "No one on."		Take a good lead off 2nd. As catcher throws to 1st, break for 3rd and beat the throw from 1st to 3rd.	
Man on 3rd	Same as "No one on."			Take a fair lead off 3rd. As catcher throws to 1st, perhaps you can beat the throw from 1st to home.
Men on 1st and 2nd	Same as "No one on."	Same as above ("Man on 1st").	You are forced. Run hard to 3rd and slide to prevent the catcher-to-3rd-to-2nd double play.	
Men on 2nd and 3rd	Same as "No one on."		Take a good lead off 2nd. As catcher throws to 1st and if 3rd-base runner goes home, break for 3rd.	Same as above ("Man on 3rd").
Men on 1st and 3rd	Same as "No one on."	Same as "Man on 1st."		Same as "Man on 3rd."
Bases loaded	Same as "No one on."	Same as "Man on 1st."	Same as "Men on 1st and 2nd."	You are forced. Hustle home and take out the catcher so he cannot complete double play at 1st. Beat the home-to-1st double play.

Note. It is assumed in all situations above that there is 0 or 1 out.

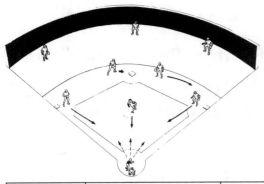

33. Bunted Ball— Slow Roller to Pitcher or 3rd or 1st

Runner's situation	Batter does:	Man on 1st does:	Man on 2nd does:	Man on 3rd does:
No one on	Run hard to 1st. Stay outside the line. Do not take the turn.			
Man on 1st	Same as above.	You are forced. Go hard for 2nd. Slide hard. Get up and be ready to go to 3rd on an overthrow at 1st.		
Man on 2nd	Same as "No one on."		Go hard for 3rd. Slide hard. Get up and be ready to go home on an overthrow at 1st.	
Man on 3rd	Same as "No one on."			If you have the lead, go hard for home. Slide hard.
Men on 1st and 2nd	Same as "No one on."	Same as above ("Man on 1st").	You are forced. Go hard for 3rd. Slide hard. Get up and be ready to go home on an overthrow at 1st.	
Men on 2nd and 3rd	Same as "No one on."		Go to 3rd fast if the 3rd-base runner breaks for home.	Same as above ("Man on 3rd").
Men on 1st and 3rd	Same as "No one on."	Same as "Man on 1st."		Same as "Man on 3rd."
Bases loaded	Same as "No one on."	Same as "Man on 1st."	Same as "Men on 1st and 2nd."	You are forced. Go hard for home. Prevent home-to-1st double play.

Note. It is assumed in all situations above that there is 0 or 1 out.

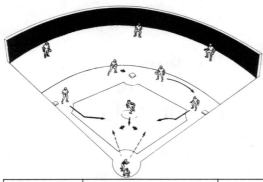

34. Bunted Ball—Good Bunt Between 3rd and Pitcher or 1st and Pitcher

Runner's situation	Batter does:	Man on 1st does:	Man on 2nd does:	Man on 3rd does:
No one on	Run hard to 1st. Run outside the line. Do not take a turn.			
Man on 1st	Same as above.	You are forced. Go into 2nd hard, sliding. Break up the 2nd-to-1st double play.		
Man on 2nd	Same as "No one on."		Go hard on the bunt. Should make it easily to 3rd. Slide hard.	
Man on 3rd	Same as "No one on."			Score on the bunt. Break for home and slide under the tag.
Men on 1st and 2nd	Same as "No one on."	Same as above ("Man on 1st").	You are forced. Go hard on the bunt. Should make it easily to 3rd. Slide hard.	
Men on 2nd and 3rd	Same as "No one on."		Go hard on the bunt. Should make it easily to 3rd. Be ready to score if ball is over-thrown at home or at 1st.	Same as above ("Man on 3rd").
Men on 1st and 3rd	Same as "No one on."	You are forced. Go into 2nd hard, sliding. Get up and be ready to go to 3rd on an over-throw at home.		Same as "Man on 3rd."
Bases loaded	Same as "No one on."	Same as above ("Men on 1st and 3rd").	You are forced. Go hard on the bunt. Should make it easily to 3rd. Be ready to score if ball is over-thrown at home.	You are forced. Score on the bunt. Break for home and slide under the tag.

Note. It is assumed in all situations above that there is 0 or 1 out.

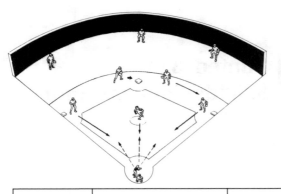

35. Bunted Ball—Hard Bunt to Pitcher or 1st or 3rd

Runner's situation	Batter does:	Man on 1st does:	Man on 2nd does:	Man on 3rd does:
No one on	Run hard to 1st, down the line. Do not round the bag. On an overthrow at 1st, be ready to go to 2nd and slide.			
Man on 1st	Run hard to 1st, down the line. Do not round the bag. On an overthrow at 1st or 2nd, be ready to go to 2nd and slide.	You are forced. Run hard to 2nd. Slide hard and try to break up the double play throw to 1st. Go on overthrow at 1st or 2nd.		
Man on 2nd	Same as "No one on."		Take a good lead off 2nd. Keep the lead and go to 3rd on a throw to 1st, or possibly score on a 1st-base overthrow.	
Man on 3rd	Same as "No one on."			Head back to 3rd, but keep a good lead. If ball is overthrown at 1st, come home sliding.
Men on 1st and 2nd	Same as "No one on."	You are forced. Run hard to 2nd, break up double play. Slide hard. Get up and be ready to advance on an overthrow.	You are forced. Run hard to 3rd, sliding. Break up the 3rd-to-1st double play.	
Men on 2nd and 3rd	Same as "No one on."		You are not forced. Take a good lead off 2nd. Be ready to go to 3rd or score on an overthrow at 1st.	You are not forced. Take a good lead off, move toward 3rd some. If ball is overthrown at 1st, come home sliding.
Men on 1st and 3rd	Same as "No one on."	Same as "Man on 1st."		Same as above ("Men on 2nd and 3rd").
Bases loaded	Run hard to 1st, down the line. Do not round the bag. Hustle to beat the home-to-1st double play.	You are forced. Run hard to 2nd and break up possible 2nd-to-1st double play. Be ready to advance on an overthrow anywhere.	You are forced. Run hard to 3rd and slide hard. Break up a possible 3rd-to-1st double play. Be ready to advance on an overthrow anywhere.	You are forced. Slide hard at home. Knock ball out of catcher's hand and prevent a home-to-1st double play.

Note. It is assumed in all situations above that there is 0 or 1 out.

36. Bunted Ball— Suicide-Squeeze Bunt

Runner's situation	Batter does:	Man on 1st does:	Man on 2nd does:	Man on 3rd does:
No one on	Impossible situation.			
Man on 1st	Impossible situation.	Impossible situation.		
Man on 2nd	Batter bunts ball near 3rd-base line. Run hard to 1st, down the line. Do not round 1st. Go to 2nd in case of overthrow at 1st or home.		*Possible play.* You must be stealing at 3rd. Just keep coming for home. Slide hard. Beat 3rd-to-1st-to-home throw. You must score!	
Man on 3rd	Same as above ("Man on 2nd").			*Possible play.* Go home on the pitch and slide hard.
Men on 1st and 2nd	Same as "Man on 2nd."	Steal on the pitch. You want to be on 3rd. Run hard to 2nd and if throw goes home or goes past 1st, go to 3rd.	Same as above ("Man on 2nd").	
Men on 2nd and 3rd	Same as "Man on 2nd."		Same as "Man on 2nd."	Same as above ("Man on 3rd").
Men on 1st and 3rd	Same as "Man on 2nd."	You want to be on 3rd. Run hard to 2nd and if throw goes home or goes past 1st, go to 3rd.		Same as "Man on 3rd."
Bases loaded	Triple steal and suicide. Bunt ball near 3rd-base line. Run hard to 1st, down the line. Go to 2nd in case of overthrow at 1st or home.	Steal on the pitch. You want to be on 3rd. Run hard to 2nd and if man ahead of you tries to score, go to 3rd.	*Possible play.* Steal on the pitch. If the double suicide sign is on, try to score. Beat 3rd-to-1st-to-home throw.	*Possible play.* Steal. Go home on the pitch and slide hard.

Note. It is assumed in all situations above that there is 0 or 1 out.

7

Baserunning Signs

The problem of signs is a controversial topic in baseball. The schools of thought on the best way to teach signs are too numerous to mention. I find that there are more coaches who favor the use of a few signs than there are who favor the use of many signals. I have always wondered why this is true, and finally I decided to ask a number of coaches about their preference for using only a few signs rather than the full number. A common response is the concern that players cannot remember more than four or five signs.

The secret to teaching a lot of signs—or anything else—is to do it in an interesting way, incorporate it into practice, and repeat it until the player masters the material. He will learn the signs if he wants to play ball badly enough.

The Total Number of Signs Required

Included at the end of this chapter is a complete list of running plays and the signs I use for them. My basic philosophy says you need a sign for every play you want to use. You never know when you will have to use them, so be ready.

I group these signs, however, so that all six bunt signs look alike, although each of the six bunt signs has one little difference that distinguishes it from the rest. My steal plays are of three very different types, so I want all signs for stealing to look very different. This helps the player avoid confusion when a steal play is on. He has a chance to think about the timing before beginning and executing the play.

Some signs may be used three or four times in a row, although others may not be used for several weeks. To keep sharp on sign-giving, -taking, and -interpretation, it is imperative that teams practice all signs as often as possible. Lack of use clouds the memory. A good method is to give all players a wallet-size card with the names of all the plays. Have players pair off in twos or threes, recite the play, and sign to each other. Never put your plays and signs together on the same paper; they could easily get lost and fall into the wrong hands.

Methods of Relaying Signs

The main consideration is not to make signs so secret the opponent can't pick them up, but to make them so simple that your team never misses one. Remember, a missed sign can cause a team to lose an out, an inning, a key game, or a championship. Sign-giving is handled in many ways. In the major leagues, the coach usually gives several, one right after the other. One sign may be the "indicator." On a particular night, for example, the team may agree to execute the third sign shown out of a series of five given. On another night it may be the second one shown. There are many possible sign systems.

In my years of coaching high school, junior high school, and American Legion baseball, I can remember only three teams out of perhaps 350 that stole my signs. These teams were kind enough to come over and tell me so after the games. An excellent system of sign-relaying some teams use is to have the spouse of a coach, a scorekeeper, or even a fan give the signs. There might have been a few instances when opponents stole a sign here or there from me, but if they did, it didn't have much impact on the outcomes of the games.

Here are two systems for relaying signs.

System A

I begin a season using only a one-sign system. I flash one sign for what I want. I hold it on until the runner and batter see it. Some teams are poor at picking up signs, so all I need to show is one sign at a time. Sometimes the other team is not even trying to steal my sign. When a team uses 12 or 13 signs instead of four or five, it is much more difficult for the opposition to steal any sign. The fewer the signs used, the easier they become to steal.

System B

If I find that I am playing against very alert opponents, or that the other team is intentionally looking for signs on every pitch, then our team goes to a four- or five-sign system. I usually give four or five signs in a row. On that day, the rule may be to execute the third sign I give. Normally, if I use the one-sign system, then giving no sign at all means hit away. If I use the multiple sign system, then we need a sign for hit away.

The Take Sign

Of all the signs in baseball, the take sign is one of the least understood and most poorly executed. It is, however, very important. The take sign tells the batter to intentionally let the ball go by. It may be given for several reasons, including the following:

- The pitcher may be weakening, and his control looks poor. Perhaps the batter can work him for a base on balls.
- Your team may be several runs behind late in the game. Players' best chance of loading the bases is to take the first few pitches to get ahead of the pitcher on every batter.
- You may call a tricky running play that requires the catcher to have the ball to start the play.
- You may have a steal play on with one or more runners. Batter is to take the pitch while runner steals a base. Swinging at the pitch could result in hitting into a fly ball double play.
- In rare cases, a fast base runner may steal home by himself. The batter takes the pitch for the safety of the runner coming home.

To execute the take command, the batter must first see the take sign given by the coach. He steps into the batter's box and takes some practice swings. The batter must give every indication that there is an intention to swing. He must not stand motionless and watch the ball whistle into the catcher's glove. Instead, the batter takes a stride, then brings the bat around halfway. This fakes out the opposing team. If there is a man on base, or if that man is stealing, the batter's half-swing and stride into the ball might hamper the catcher's vision, causing him to drop the ball, slow up his throw to the base, or make an inaccurate throw. If the batter stands motionless when taking a pitch, this gives the catcher a full view of the field and does not assist the runner at all.

The Wipeoff Sign

The wipeoff sign is very important to coaches and players on offense. It can be given for several reasons:

- The coach may have had second thoughts and not want the team to go through with a play. Coaches make mental errors, but the wipeoff sign rectifies them.
- The coach or someone on your team may notice the opposing team has picked up one of the team's signs. When the opponent steals signs and moves in such a way that the play will surely fail, then the wipeoff sign is imperative.
- The coach may have given a sign and his team is ready to execute it. Suddenly, he realizes another play will work even better. He wipes off the old play and gives the sign for the new play.
- The wipeoff sign should be very fast and simple. I usually wipe my hand across the letters on my uniform, as if I were wiping dirt off my hands.

Whenever a sign is given, as soon as the pitch is made and the batter does not hit the ball and the runners do not move, another sign must be given. Players should never assume that a sign is given for the duration of that batter's time at bat. A new sign must be given to the batter and each runner after each pitch. For this reason, it is vital that batters look for a sign after every pitch in the game. Runners should go back to their base and take a long, hard look before moving off again.

When a Sign Is Misunderstood or Missed

If at any time a player does not understand a sign, he should call for a time-out immediately. As soon as the player is given time by the umpire, he should meet with the coach and receive the sign verbally, using as much time as allowed. However, if the person giving the sign feels the time-out request might tell the defensive team what is coming next, then the wipeoff sign should be given, or the coach should tell the player during the time-out that the sign is off. When the players return to their positions, before the umpire yells, "Play ball," the person giving the sign may give another sign and start a new play.

Table 7.1 Running Plays and Signs

Sign	Name of play	Visual	Verbal	Signal	Special tips
	Drag bunt or sacrifice bunt (move runner only one base) or suicide squeeze (score one run)	X		Coach puts one hand on one knee: Hand on left knee means bunt left side of diamond. Hand on right knee means bunt right side of diamond.	Same sign to batter and runner. Same sign to runner only if he is on 3rd.
	Safe-squeeze bunt	X		Coach tugs at his belt with one or two hands.	Same sign to batter and runner. No steal sign to runner.

(Cont.)

Table 7.1 Running Plays and Signs (Cont.)

Sign	Name of play	Visual	Verbal	Signal	Special tips
	Suicide squeeze (score two runs) or sacrifice bunt man from 1st to 3rd	X		Coach puts two hands on two knees.	Same sign to batter and two runners. Also give all runners sign to steal on the pitch.
	Fake bunt and steal 2nd or 3rd	X		To runners: Coach puts hand to face area. To batter: Coach shows closed fist.	This play requires two signs. Steal sign given to runners.
	Fake bunt and slash (man on 1st, 2nd, or 3rd)	X		Coach moves hand from neck to crotch, straight down.	Same sign to batter and runner. No steal sign to runners.
	Take sign	X		Coach folds arms across chest.	Same sign to runners and batters. Runner may receive steal sign.

(Cont.)

Table 7.1 Running Plays and Signs (Cont.)

Sign	Name of play	Visual	Verbal	Signal	Special tips
	Hit and run play	X		To batter: Coach crosses legs—sitting or standing. To runners: Coach puts hand in face area.	This play requires two signs. Runners receive steal sign.
	Single steal on pitcher	X		Coach puts hand to face or neck area (all four plays).	Same sign for all four plays—batter picks up same sign. Batter gets take sign on steal home play.
	Double steal on pitcher	X			
	Triple steal on pitcher (man on 3rd)	X			
	Steal home on pitcher.	X			
	Delay steal (man on 2nd, 1st and 2nd, 2nd and 3rd)	X		To runner: Coach waves arm in front of him horizontally to indicate "no, no."	Batter is not involved (hit away). Take may be given.
	Delay steal (bases loaded)	X		To runners: Coach waves arm in front of him horizontally to indicate "no, no."	Batter is not involved, or take sign may be given.

(Cont.)

Table 7.1 Running Plays and Signs (Cont.)

Sign	Name of play	Visual	Verbal	Signal	Special tips
	Fake steal play	X		Coach kicks the dirt with either foot.	Batter and runner get same sign. Batter may swing.
	Double steal before the pitch with men on 1st and 3rd (0 or 1 out)	X	X	Coach yells "ok" and the last name of 1st-base runner. He then yells the correct number of outs.\n\nCoach will motion.	
	Double steal before the pitch with men on 1st and 3rd (2 outs)		X	Coach yells "ok" and the last name of 1st-base runner. He then yells "two away."	Batter is not involved. 3rd-base runner off base a little.
	Double steal before the pitch with men on 3rd and batter at plate	X	X	In time-out, coach tells batter who walks: jog to 1st, count "1001," adjust belt, dash for 2nd. Coach motions 3rd-base runner off the base a little.	Two signs are required for this play.
	Double steal on the pitch with men on 1st and 3rd (any number of outs)	X		To 1st-base runner: Coach puts hand to face or neck area. Coach motions 3rd-base runner off the base a little.	Two signs are required for this play.

(Cont.)

Table 7.1 Running Plays and Signs (Cont.)

Sign	Name of play	Visual	Verbal	Signal	Special tips
	Double steal after the pitch with men on 1st and 3rd (any number of outs)	X		To 1st-base runner: Coach gives delayed steal sign (moves hand across body horizontally). Coach motions 3rd-base runner off the base a little.	Two signs are required for this play.

Play Selector

Early in my coaching career I developed a play selector (in notebook form) that would give me ready reference to all the offensive options I had learned. Each time a different running situation existed, I could flip the notebook to the proper section under which would be listed all the possible plays available for that situation.

I placed the notebook in a light plastic cover with two hooks at the top and attached a metal rod to the bottom of it. When a game started, I would hook this device on the fence or dugout where I could stand and see it (Figure A.1).

The notebook contained eight pages, one for each possible combination of men on base. On each situation page, I listed three sections: "0 out," "1 out," "2 outs." Across the top of each page I listed the six categories of plays I used most often, in the order in which I was most likely to use them. This made it possible for me to scan each page quickly to make the appropriate play selection.

Using the Play Selector

As soon as a play has ended and the pitcher has the ball, flip to the page in the selector for the number of runners currently on the bases. On that page, look at the section that shows the correct number of outs. As your eye scans from left to right, you see every available play for this situation. The plays on the left are the ones called most often. Quickly

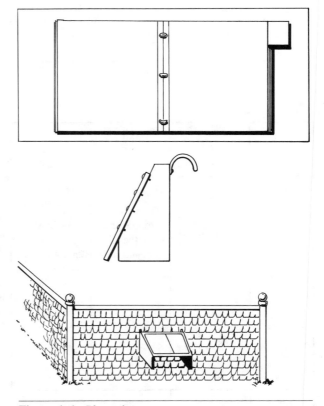

Figure A.1 Play selector.

choose the play you want, flash the sign, and the play is on. Then as play continues and circumstances change, you can easily flip to another page.

Use this tool for review between games. Add some plays of your own and delete the plays you are less likely to use. A sample selector is provided on the next few pages.

No One on Base

	Hit away	Hit and run	Fake bunt	Bunt	Steal on pitch	Steal before pitch	Delay steal
0 out	Hit away Base on balls Hit by pitcher	No	Fake bunt, slash over 1st or 3rd or through a hole	Drag bunt for a base hit	No	No	No
1 out	Same as above	No	Same as above	Same as above	No	No	No
2 outs	Same as above	No	No	Same as above	No	No	No

Man on 1st

	Hit away	Hit and run	Fake bunt	Bunt	Steal on pitch	Steal before pitch	Delay steal
0 out	Hit away Base on balls Hit by pitcher	Hit and run Batter hits through or over the opposite hole	Fake bunt and steal 2nd Fake bunt and steal 2nd. Batter slash over 1st or 3rd	Drag bunt for a hit between 1st and pitcher or down 3rd-base line Sacrifice bunt—move runner 1 or 2 bases Third strike bunt and steal or hold	Steal on pitcher and batter takes Steal on pitcher and batter swings	No	No
1 out	Same as above	Same as above	Same as above	Same as above	Same as above	No	No
2 outs	Same as above	Same as above	Same as above	Drag bunt for a hit between 1st and pitcher or down 3rd-base line No sacrifice bunts	A steal situation Take or swing	No	No

Man on 2nd

	Hit away	Hit and run	Fake bunt	Bunt	Steal on pitch	Steal before pitch	Delay steal
0 out	Hit away Base on balls Hit by pitcher	Hit and run Batter hits through or over the opposite hole	Fake bunt and steal 3rd Batter slash over 1st or 3rd	Sacrifice bunt—move the runner 1 or 2 bases along Drag bunt between pitcher and 3rd 3rd strike bunt	Steal on the pitch—batter takes or swings	No	Delay steal on catcher's throw to 2nd or pitcher
1 out	Same as above	Same as above	Same as above	Same as above	Same as above	No	Same as above
2 outs	Same as above	Same as above	No	Surprise drag bunt for a base hit and move the runner to 3rd	Steal 3rd if you have a big lead	No	Same as above

Man on 3rd

	Hit away	Hit and run	Fake bunt	Bunt	Steal on pitch	Steal before pitch	Delay steal
0 out	Hit away Base on balls Hit by pitcher	No hit and run Work for sacrifice fly deep	Fake bunt and slash over 3rd or 1st	Drag bunt down 3rd- or 1st-base line to get on base and runner holds up Safe squeeze Suicide squeeze Third strike bunt	Steal home on pitcher on the catcher's throw back to the pitcher	No	Delay steal on catcher's throw to 3rd
1 out	Same as above	Same as above	Same as above	Same as above	Same as above	No	Same as above
2 outs	Same as above	No	No	Drag bunt down 3rd- or 1st-base line and runner holds up Safe squeeze Suicide squeeze	Only in desperation	No	Delay steal on catcher's throw to 3rd or on catcher's throw back to pitcher

Men on 1st and 2nd

	Hit away	Hit and run	Fake bunt	Bunt	Steal on pitch	Steal before pitch	Delay steal
0 out	Hit away Base on balls Hit by pitcher	Hit and run through the opposite hole (this may develop into a triple play on line drive fly)	Batter fake bunts and only runner on 2nd steals to 3rd Batter fake bunts and both runners steal Fake bunt slash over 1st or 3rd Runners play it safe	This is automatic bunt situation. Sacrifice bunt one or two bases Suicide bunt from 2nd to home Drag bunt to get on, runners go Third strike bunt	Steal on the pitch to 3rd and 2nd if the 3rd-baseman plays in too far	No	Delay steal with men on 1st and 2nd Delay steal on catcher's throw back to pitcher
1 out	Same as above	Same as above	Same as above	Same as above	Steal on the pitch to 3rd and 2nd if the 3rd-baseman plays in too far	No	Same as above
2 outs	Same as above	Hit and run through the opposite hole (with 2 outs there is no danger of double or triple play)	No	Drag bunt to get on	Steal on pitcher—move runners to 2nd and 3rd Steal 2nd, runner only to 3rd, then run 1st and 3rd plays with 2 outs	No	Delay steal with men on 1st and 2nd If you have a big lead, delay steal on catcher's throw to pitcher

Men on 2nd and 3rd

	Hit away	Hit and run	Fake bunt	Bunt	Steal on pitch	Steal before pitch	Delay steal
0 out	Hit away Base on balls Hit by pitcher Sacrifice fly	No	Fake bunt and slash over 1st- or 3rd-base hole—runners play it safe	Drag bunt Safe-squeeze bunt Suicide-squeeze bunt score 1 or 2 runs	Steal home on pitcher's delivery—both runners steal	No	Delay steal at home on the catcher's throw to pitcher Delay-steal play with men on 2nd and 3rd
1 out	Same as above	No	Same as above	Same as above	Same as above	No	Same as above
2 outs	Hit away Base on balls Hit by pitcher	No	No	No	Same as above	No	Same as above

Men on 1st and 3rd

	Hit away	Hit and run	Fake bunt	Bunt	Steal on pitch	Steal before pitch	Delay steal
0 out	Hit away Base on balls Hit by pitcher Sacrifice fly	Hit and run through or over opposite hole—1st-base runner goes but 3rd-base runner plays it safe and can hold up or score	Fake bunt and slash over 1st- or 3rd-base hole—1st-base runner steals and 3rd-base runner plays it safe Fake bunt—1st-base runner steals and 3rd-base runner holds up	Drag bunt to get on Safe-squeeze bunt Suicide-squeeze bunt and score 1 run Third strike bunt	Steal 2nd base—3rd-base runner holds Steal 2nd—3rd-base runner scores on throw to 2nd Steal 2nd and home on pitcher	Double steal on the early steal play Double steal on the early steal but play starts at home when batter walks	Double steal on catcher's throw back to pitcher. Both runners steal Double steal as 3rd-base runner works a delay steal on catcher's throw to 3rd
1 out	Same as above	Same as above	Same as above	Same as above	Same as above	Same as above	Same as above
2 outs	Same as above	Same as above	No	No	Same as above	Same as above	Delay steal on the catcher's throw to pitcher only if you have a big lead and fast 3rd-base runner

Bases Loaded

	Hit away	Hit and run	Fake bunt	Bunt	Steal on pitch	Steal before pitch	Delay steal
0 out	Hit away Base on balls Hit by pitcher	Do not hit and run but work for sacrifice fly deep	Fake bunt and slash over 3rd or 1st	Suicide-squeeze bunt—score 1 or 2 runs Warning: Possible double or triple play on pop-up	Steal on pitcher if you have a big lead, fast 3rd-base runner, and pitcher winds up	No	Delay steal on catcher's throw to 3rd or to pitcher Use these only if you have big lead and fast runner
1 out	Same as above	Same as above	Same as above	Same as above	Same as above	No	Same as above
2 outs	Same as above	No	No	No	Same as above	No	No

Glossary

Aboard: On base.

Advance: To go from one base to another in correct order.

At the corners: Having two base runners only, at first and third base.

Automatic take: At the three balls and no strikes count, the batter takes the pitch unless given the green light to swing.

Away: Out. *One away* means one out.

Back through the box: A ball hit back directly through the pitcher's box. The term usually denotes a ground ball that may be fielded by the pitcher or may go through for a base hit.

Bag: One of the three bases, other than home plate, on the diamond.

Balk: Movement by the pitcher in which each runner is awarded one base advancement.

Ball: Pitch that does not pass through the strike zone at home plate.

Base hit: Any hit in which the runner safely reaches the base without error or fielder's choice.

Base on balls: Four balls thrown by the pitcher, entitling the batter to gain first base.

Base path: Strip of space between bases in which the runner must stay while advancing from base to base.

Base runner: Any player who is on base or running the base paths after hitting a fair ball or being awarded first base.

Bases empty: When no base is occupied by a runner.

Bases loaded: When first, second, and third bases are occupied by runners.

BB: In score keeping, an abbreviation for a batter's "base on balls."

Beat out: To hustle down the first-base line and arrive at first base before the infielder's throw.

Behind in the count: Counts that are in favor of the batter. Some examples include "three and oh [zero]," "two and oh," and "three and one."

Blast: A very long, hard hit, usually referring to a triple or a home run.

Bleeder: A softly hit ball that just barely goes past or between infielders for a base hit. It may be a slow roller that dies halfway down the third-base line, a dribbler that finds its way through the infield, or a weakly hit pop fly that drops in front of an outfielder.

Bloop, blooper: A short, soft fly that usually drops in for a base hit just beyond the infield.

Box: The area where the base coach, catcher, or batter must stay.

Bring in: To score another runner.

Bunt: The act of softly hitting a pitched ball so it dribbles away from the plate.

Call: Either a ball or a strike on a pitch at home plate or a decision in the field during play.

Catch him leaning: A pitcher's throw to a base when a player has led off too far and cannot get back to that base.

Circuit clout: Home run.

Clean the bases: Act of hitting a single, double, triple, or home run that drives in all runners.

Cleanup: That number-four hitter in a baseball lineup who is a power or long-ball hitter.

Coach's box: Designated areas near first base and third base where coaches must stay.

Connected: Hit the ball well.

Corner bag: Either the first- or third-base bag.

Count: The number of balls and strikes called on the batter.

Courtesy runner: Runner allowed, by the rules, to run for a batter who has reached a base.

Crossover: The first step a runner takes when starting toward the next base.

Cut down: When a runner is thrown out before reaching the next base.

Daylight: The distance between a runner and the base when leading off before a pitch.

Delayed double steal: A play in which, with runners at first and third, the runner at first base breaks for second in an attempt to steal. If the catcher throws to second, the runner at third tries to steal home.

Delayed steal: Any steal executed by a running team in which the runners go after the catcher receives the pitch.

Die: When a runner is left stranded on base at the end of an inning.

Dish: A term referring only to home plate.

Double: A two-base hit in which the batter safely reaches second base.

Double steal: When two base runners steal on the same called play.

Double up: To make an out on the batter and on a runner in the same play.

Down the line: A ball hit down the first- or third-base line, or a runner who goes between the two chalk lines to first base.

Drag: A quick, short, soft bunt that dies near the third- or first-base line. Drag usually refers to a bunt that is laid down softly while the bunter attempts to reach first base.

Drag bunt: Because the left-handed batter has a step or more advantage over the right-hander in breaking toward first base, this term refers to the left-handed batter bunting down the first- or third-base line very slowly and trying to beat the throw to first base.

Earned run: The act of a batter driving in a runner with a hit ball or a walk.

Edge off: Gradually creeping farther and farther off a base.

Extra base hit: Any double, triple, or home run hit by a batter.

Fake steal: When a runner makes a body or leg motion as if to run to the next base, but stops and comes back to the original base.

Fielder's choice: When a runner gains first base because a fielder made a play at another base.

Force: Runners who are out at a base because all other bases behind them are occupied by runners.

Forceout: An out caused by a force. The runner need not be tagged with the ball.

Foul ball: Any ball that lands outside the foul lines after it is hit.

Foul territory: The territory outside the foul lines and up to the grandstands.

Foul tip: Batted ball caught in the air by the catcher in foul territory. Runners may advance on the pitch.

Free pass: An intentional walk.

Full count: Three balls and two strikes on the hitter.

Gap shot: A base hit, a double or triple, driven deep in the gap between two outfielders. It will usually roll to the outfield wall.

Give oneself up: When a runner sacrifices himself as an out for the good of the team score.

Go with the pitch: When a batter tries to hit the ball to the side of the diamond that is natural for that type of pitch.

Green light: A signal from a coach allowing a batter to hit away rather than take the next pitch, or the signal from a coach allowing a base runner to attempt to steal the next base.

Ground out: When a batter causes an out by hitting the ball on the ground.

Grounder: A ball hit on the ground.

Ground rule double: When a batted ball hits the ground and bounces into outfield grandstands, the batter is awarded two bases and all runners advance two bases.

Hit and run: A play in which the first-base runner breaks for second base, as though stealing, and the batter is obligated to hit the ball to protect the runner.

Hit behind the runner: A batter hits the ball to the first-base side of the diamond when the runner runs ahead of the ball.

Hit for distance: To hit the ball as far from the plate as possible.

Hit the dirt: Slide.

Hold at second base: To stop or stay at second base.

Infield fly rule: A special rule to protect base runners. It applies only when runners are on first and second base or when bases are loaded. If a fair fly is hit in infield fly territory, the batter is automatically out and all runners on base advance at their own peril.

Infield hit: Any ball hit within the infield, even if it results in a base hit.

Infield out: Any out made by a batter when the ball is fielded in the infield.

Intentional walk: When a pitcher awards first base to a batter by purposely throwing four balls.

Interference—offensive: When a batter, runner, or base coach interferes with a defensive player fielding a ball. This can occur when a base coach touches or assists a runner.

Interference—defensive: When a defensive player interferes with the action of the offense.

In the hole: In the area of ground to the right and deep behind the shortstop. Any good shortstop must cover this area well.

Jump: When a base runner takes more of a lead than the pitcher should have allowed. The good jump greatly assists the runner in stealing the next base.

K: Symbol that designates a strikeout when keeping a scorecard.

Lay it down: To bunt a ball on the ground.

Lead: The number of steps that a runner gets off the base before the pitch.

Lead-off: First position in the batting order, usually taken by a player who hits well, is generally a singles hitter, has a knack for drawing walks, and runs the bases well.

Leave men on: At the end of the inning, to have runners still on bases who did not score.

Leg it out: To run hard to first base after hitting the ball.

Line call: A ball hit right on the first- or third-base line that could be either fair or foul.

Load 'em up: To fill the bases.

Long ball: Fly ball hit far from the plate.

Long count: Count of three balls and two strikes.

Obstruction: When a player places himself in front of another player, preventing a play.

On base: A runner who has earned his way from one base to another.

Opposite field: Field opposite to which a hitter normally hits.

Overslide: To slide beyond the base.

Payoff pitch: A pitch with a full count. The next pitch must pay off (if not fouled off) in a walk, strikeout, or a ball in fair play.

Pickoff: A pitcher's or catcher's throw to a base in an attempt to tag a runner who is off the base.

Pick up a man: When a hitter knocks a base runner in for a score.

Pinch runner: A player from the bench who comes in and runs for a man on base.

Pop-up: High, lazy fly ball that takes a long time to come down.

Power: Ability to hit a ball a long distance.

Ribby, ribbies (RBI):   Run batted in. When a batter causes a player to score a run within the rules.

Rookie: First-year player or one who has played sparingly in a previous season.

Rundown: When a runner is trapped between two bases and eventually is tagged with the ball.

Sacrifice hit: Occurs when a batter lays down a bunt to successfully move a runner one base further. The batter is thrown out at first base.

Sacrifice fly: Occurs when a batter lifts a high fly to the outfield. A player from third base scores before the outfield throw comes home.

Scoring position: When a runner has reached second or third base.

Send: To allow or signal a runner to go to the next base as the pitch is delivered to the plate.

Sign: A signal that a coach gives to a player who is on the field or at bat indicating a particular play is in effect.

Single: One-base hit.

Slash: To bring the bat behind the shoulder, then forward with an abbreviated swing.

Slice: A ball hit in such a manner that it spins excessively and curves; the reaction depends on whether it was hit by a right- or left-handed batter.

Slide: The act of going to a base by throwing one's body to the ground before arrival.

Squeeze: The squeeze or safe squeeze occurs when the third-base runner slides home on a bunt, only if the runner sees that the bunt is safely down on the ground providing the opportunity to score safely.

Suicide squeeze: A planned play in which the base runner on third breaks with the pitch, as if trying to steal home. At the same time, the batter tries to execute a successful bunt, enabling the runner to score. The runner goes regardless.

Steal: To run from base to base without the defense throwing you out and with no help from the batter.

Stranded: A runner who is left on base without scoring at the end of an inning.

Strawberry: A type of open sore, which is very painful and slow to heal, on the body or leg of a sliding base runner. Sliding pads usually prevent this.

Swing away: The action of a batter unless signaled by the coach to take or to bunt.

Tag: To touch some part of a runner's body with the ball.

Tag up: To stay on a base until a fly ball is caught, then proceed to the next base.

Take: Rather than swinging, the batter lets the pitch go by.

Triple: Three-base hit.

Triple play: Any continuous play by the defense in which three successive outs are made.

Unearned run: Any run caused by an error of the defense.

Walk: A batter goes from home plate to first base after receiving four balls from the pitcher.

Bibliography

Honig, D. (1981). *The Brooklyn Dodgers: An illustrated tribute.* New York: St. Martin's.

Kindall, J. (1983). *Sports Illustrated baseball.* New York: Harper and Row.

Kraft, J.A. (1983). Slide, man, slide. *Letterman,* pp. 41-43.

Leib, F. (1977). *Baseball as I have known it.* New York: Coward, McCann, & Geoghegan.

National Baseball Congress of America. (1987). *Official baseball rules.* Wichita, KS: Author.

National Federation of State High School Athletic Associations. (1986). *The official baseball rule book.* Elgin, IL: Author.

Office of Commissioner of Baseball. (1988). *Official baseball rules.* New York: Author.

Reichler, J. (1979). *Baseball's great moments.* New York: Crown.

Schoor, G. (1984). *The complete Dodgers record book.* New York: Facts on File.

Siwoff, S. (Ed.). (1982). *The book of baseball records.* New York: Author.

Turkin, H., & Thompson, S.C. (1976). *The official baseball encyclopedia.* New York: A. S. Barnes.

Tygiel, J. (1983). *Baseball's great experiment: Jackie Robinson and his legacy.* New York: Oxford University Press.

Webster's sports dictionary. (1976). Springfield, MA: Merriam-Webster.

References

Kindall, J. (1983). *Sports Illustrated baseball*. New York: Harper and Row.

National Baseball Congress of America. (1987). *Official baseball rules*. Wichita, KS: Author.

Index

A

Appeal plays
  offensive, 87
  defensive, 88

B

Balk, by pitcher, 74, 85, 86, 111
Balls hit
  36 types defined, 117-154
Baseline, defined, 78
Base, touching, 73-74, 84-85
Baserunning. *See also* Running bases
  equipment, 7
  factors influencing, 6
  myths and fallacies, 5, 6
Baserunning plays, charts
  before, on, after pitcher's delivery, 11
  by positions of runners, 10
  by types of offensive men involved, 12
Baserunning rules
  for bunted balls, 92, 149-154
  for fair fly balls, 118, 120-133
  for foul fly balls, 118, 119, 123
  for ground balls, 117, 118, 134-148
Baserunning times, 13
Blocking the plate, by the catcher, 98
Bunting plays
  drag bunt for a hit, 52-53
  sacrifice bunt, move runners one base, 4, 54-55
  sacrifice bunt, move runners two bases, 56-57
  safe squeeze bunt, 58-59
  suicide squeeze bunt, score one run, 60-61
  suicide squeeze bunt, score two runs, 62-63

C

Carew, Rod, 105
Cartwright, Alexander, 1
Catcher, characteristics of, 106
Cincinnati Red Stockings, 1
Cobb, Ty, 105
Coleman, Vince, 5
Crossover step, runner's, 108

D

Doubleday, Abner, 1
Double, ground rule, 76

Double plays
  breaking up, shortstop, and second base type, 94-95
  reverse type, 79
Double steal plays. *See* Steal plays
Drills, baserunning, 73-85

F

Fake bunt and slash plays
  with man on first or second base, 64-65
  with man on third base, 66-67
Fake bunting plays
  with a man on first base, 70-71
  with a man on second base, 68-69
Fake steal play, 50-51, 113
First-base coach, 87
  instructions to, 93-94
First run of the game
  six methods of scoring, 101-103
Four dimensions of offensive strategy, xi, 2

H

Henderson, Rickey, 105
Hidden-ball trick, 94, 99
Hit and run play, 2, 47-49
Home run, defined, 75

I

Infield fly rule, 86-87
Intentional walk, 98-99
Interference, offensive or defensive types
  catcher's interference, 75, 78
  hitter's interference, 80, 81-84
  player's, 85
  runner's, 78, 81-84

K

Kindall, Jerry, 4, 40

L

Left on base (LOB), 3

M

Martin, Pepper, 105
McGee, Willie, 5
Missed third strike, by catcher, 92
Multiple runner plays, 4

N

National Association of Baseball Players, 1
Negative statistics, baseball, 3
New York Yankees, 5

O

Obstruction, rules for
  on the batter, 77-78
  on the runner, 77-78
Offensive baseball, four dimensions, xi, 2
One-and-One Rule, baseball overthrows, 77
Overrunning bases, 81, 84
Oversliding bases, 81, 84
Overthrows by pitchers, 77

P

Passed balls, 97
Pickoff plays
  by the catcher, 93-97
  by the pitcher, 93-97
Pitcher's balk. *See* Balk
Pitcher's characteristics, 105-106
Pitches, wild, 97
Play selector, offensive coaching device, 163-168
Play selector charts, 164-168
  bases loaded, 168
  man on first base, 164
  man on second base, 165
  man on third base, 165
  men on first and second bases, 166
  men on first and third bases, 167
  men on second and third bases, 167
  no men on bases, 164
Purists, baseball, 2, 4

R

Raines, Tim, 105
Robinson, Jackie, 5, 105
Rounders, British game, 1
Runner
  assisting a scoring runner, 98
  following, 74
  hit by batted ball, 24, 80
  passing another runner, 80
  preceding, 74
  rundown rules, 99
Running bases
  first base to second base, 93-95
  home to first base, 89-93

  second base to third base, 95-96
  third base to home, 96-98
Running form
  actual run, 90-91
  approach to the base, 92
  taking the first-base turn, 107-108
  taking the first step, 89-90
Running, rules, 73-88
Running, types of leadoffs, 108-116
  the primary leads, 108-109, 111-116
  the secondary leads, 108, 111-116

S

Safe squeeze play. *See* Squeeze plays
Signals, baserunning, 155-161
  charts for signs and plays of offense, 157-161
  methods of relaying, 155-156
  missed and misunderstood signs, 157
  number required, 155
Single steals. *See* Steal plays
Sliding instructions, 100-101
Squeeze plays, 97
Statistics, positive and negative baseball, 3
Steal plays, double steal type
  before the pitch, men on first base and third base, with none or one out, 15-18, 97
  before the pitch, men on first base and third base, with two outs, 15-18, 97
  before the pitch, man on third base and batter walks, 19-20
  delayed, on catcher's throwback, men on first and second bases, 39-40
  delayed, on catcher's throwback, men on second and third bases, 41-42
  delayed, on catcher's throwback, men on first and third bases, none or one out, 33-34
  delayed, on catcher's throwback, men on first and third bases, with two outs, 35-36
  on pitcher's delivery, men on first base and second base, 23-24
  on pitcher's delivery, men on first base and third base, with none or one out, 29-30, 97
  on pitcher's delivery, men on first base and third base, with two outs, 31-32
Steal plays, fake, 113
Steal plays, the five categories
  delayed, catcher's throw to a base, 108, 110
  delayed, catcher's throw to pitcher, 110
  delayed, pitcher's throw to a base, 108

early, before pitcher's delivery, 15-20, 97
straight, on pitcher's delivery, 108, 110-111
Steal plays, on the pitcher at each base
  stealing home, 113-116
  stealing second base, 108-111
  stealing third base, 111-113
Steal plays, single steal type
  delayed, on catcher's throwback, man on second
    base, 37-38
  delayed, on catcher's throwback, man on third
    base, 45-46
  on pitcher's delivery, man on first base or second
    base, 21-22
  on pitcher's delivery, man on third base, 27-28
Steal plays, triple steal type
  delayed, on catcher's throwback, bases loaded,
    43-44
  on pitcher's delivery, bases loaded, 25-26

Stolen base, defined, 86
Suicide squeeze play. *See* Squeeze plays

T

Tagging up, fly ball rules, 84
Take sign, 156
Third-base coach, instructions to, 87, 97-98
Touching bases. *See* Base
Triple steal plays. *See* Steal plays

W

Whip plays
  from an outfield hit, 94
  from a successful sacrifice bunt, 94
Wild pitches. *See* Pitches
Wills, Maury, 105
Wipeoff sign, 156
Wooden, John, 5